THE HOBBIT

J. R. R. Tolkien

SPARK PUBLISHING

SPARKNOTES is a registered trademark of SparkNotes LLC

Spark Publishing
A Division of Barnes & Noble
120 Fifth Avenue
New York, NY 10011
www.sparknotes.com

ISBN-13: 978-1-4114-0380-2
ISBN-10: 1-4114-0380-0

Please submit changes or report errors to www.sparknotes.com/errors.

Printed in the United States.

10 9 8 7 6 5 4

CONTENTS

CONTEXT

JOHN RONALD REUEL TOLKIEN WAS BORN on January 3, 1892, in Bloemfontain, South Africa. His parents had moved there from England so that his father, Arthur, could work for the bank of Africa. Tolkien lost both parents early in life—his father died in Africa in 1896 after the rest of the family had returned to England, and his mother, Mabel, died in 1904 near Birmingham, England. After Mabel's death, Tolkien and his younger brother, Hilary, came under the care of Father Francis Morgan, a friend of the family's. Soon after, Tolkien went to King Edward's School and then to Oxford.

At Oxford, Tolkien pursued a degree in English language and literature. He developed a particular passion for philology, the study of languages. While studying Old English, Anglo-Saxon, and Welsh poetry, he continued experimenting with a language of his own, which he had started to do in his youth. This language would form the groundwork for his imagined world known as Middle-Earth.

By 1916, Tolkien had received his degree and married his childhood sweetheart, Edith Bratt. He eventually took a teaching position at Oxford. By 1929, he had had his fourth child with Edith. During these years, he also began his great mythology of Middle-Earth, a compendium of stories called *The Silmarillion*. Out of these stories grew *The Hobbit* (1936), his first published work. A simple children's story about a small person who takes part in great adventures, the novel's playful tone and imagery made it a hit both with children and adults. *The Hobbit*'s success also gave Tolkien a huge public that was anxious to learn more about the meticulously developed world that he had created around his invented language and mythology, only a small part of which was detailed in *The Hobbit*.

The Hobbit's plot and characters combined the ancient heroic Anglo-Saxon and Scandinavian epics Tolkien studied with the middle-class rural England in which he lived. In many ways, the novel's charm and humor lie in transplanting a simple, pastoral Englishman of the 1930s into a heroic medieval setting. Tolkien acknowledged that his hero, Bilbo Baggins, was patterned on the rural Englishmen of his own time.

By the time Tolkien began to work on the sequel to *The Hobbit*, he had developed a friendship with another well-known Oxford professor and writer, C. S. Lewis, author of *The Chronicles of Narnia*. Their friendship lasted for many years. Tolkien helped convert Lewis to Christianity (although Tolkien, a Roman Catholic, was disappointed that Lewis became a Protestant), and the two critiqued each other's work as part of an informal group of writers known as the Inklings.

From 1945 to 1959, Tolkien continued to teach at Oxford and wrote *The Lord of the Rings* trilogy, which served as a follow-up to *The Hobbit*. The trilogy brought Tolkien fame in England and America, but he was never a public figure. He continued work on *The Silmarillion* and other tales and led a quiet life. Despite his public acclaim, he was most comfortable with middle-class surroundings and peace in which to write and think. Tolkien died on September 2, 1973. *The Silmarillion* was edited and published posthumously by his son Christopher in 1977.

PLOT OVERVIEW

Bilbo BAGGINS LIVES a quiet, peaceful life in his comfortable hole at Bag End. Bilbo lives in a hole because he is a hobbit—one of a race of small, plump people about half the size of humans, with furry toes and a great love of good food and drink. Bilbo is quite content at Bag End, near the bustling hobbit village of Hobbiton, but one day his comfort is shattered by the arrival of the old wizard Gandalf, who persuades Bilbo to set out on an adventure with a group of thirteen militant dwarves. The dwarves are embarking on a great quest to reclaim their treasure from the marauding dragon Smaug, and Bilbo is to act as their "burglar." The dwarves are very skeptical about Gandalf's choice for a burglar, and Bilbo is terrified to leave his comfortable life to seek adventure. But Gandalf assures both Bilbo and the dwarves that there is more to the little hobbit than meets the eye.

Shortly after the group sets out, three hungry trolls capture all of them except for Gandalf. Gandalf tricks the trolls into remaining outside when the sun comes up, and the sunlight turns the nocturnal trolls to stone. The group finds a great cache of weapons in the trolls' camp. Gandalf and the dwarf lord Thorin take magic swords, and Bilbo takes a small sword of his own.

The group rests at the elfish stronghold of Rivendell, where they receive advice from the great elf lord Elrond, then sets out to cross the Misty Mountains. When they find shelter in a cave during a snowstorm, a group of goblins who live in the caverns beneath the mountain take them prisoner. Gandalf leads the dwarves to a passage out of the mountain, but they accidentally leave behind Bilbo.

Wandering through the tunnels, Bilbo finds a strange golden ring lying on the ground. He takes the ring and puts it in his pocket. Soon he encounters Gollum, a hissing, whining creature who lives in a pool in the caverns and hunts fish and goblins. Gollum wants to eat Bilbo, and the two have a contest of riddles to determine Bilbo's fate. Bilbo wins by asking the dubious riddle, "What have I got in my pocket?"

Gollum wants to eat Bilbo anyway, and he disappears to fetch his magic ring, which turns its wearer invisible. The ring, however, is the same one Bilbo has already found, and Bilbo uses it to escape from Gollum and flee the goblins. He finds a tunnel leading up out of the mountain and discovers that the dwarves and Gandalf have already escaped. Evil wolves known as Wargs pursue them, but Bilbo and his comrades are helped to safety by a group of great eagles and by Beorn, a creature who can change shape from a man into a bear.

The company enters the dark forest of Mirkwood, and, making matters worse, Gandalf abandons them to see to some other urgent business. In the forest, the dwarves are caught in the webs of some giant spiders, and Bilbo must rescue them with his sword and magic ring. After slaying his first spider, Bilbo names his sword Sting. Shortly after escaping the spiders, the unlucky dwarves are captured by a group of wood elves who live near the river that runs through Mirkwood. Bilbo uses his ring to help the company escape and slips the dwarves away from the elves by hiding them inside barrels, which he then floats down the river. The dwarves arrive at Lake Town, a human settlement near the Lonely Mountain, under which the great dragon sleeps with Thorin's treasure.

After sneaking into the mountain, Bilbo talks to the sly dragon Smaug, who unwittingly reveals that his armorlike scales have a weak spot near his heart. When Bilbo steals a golden cup from the dragon's hoard, Smaug is furious and flies out of the mountain to burn Lake Town in his rage. Bard, a heroic archer, has learned the secret about Smaug's weakness from a thrush, and he fires an arrow into the dragon's heart, killing him. Before Smaug dies, however, he burns Lake Town to the ground.

The humans of Lake Town and the elves of Mirkwood march to the Lonely Mountain to seek a share of the treasure as compensation for their losses and aid, but Thorin greedily refuses, and the humans and elves besiege the mountain, trapping the dwarves and the hobbit inside. Bilbo sneaks out to join the humans in an attempt to bring peace. When Thorin learns what Bilbo has done, he is livid, but Gandalf suddenly reappears and saves Bilbo from the dwarf lord's wrath.

At this moment, an army of goblins and Wargs marches on the mountain, and the humans, elves, and dwarves are forced to band together to defeat them. The goblins nearly win, but the arrival of Beorn and the eagles helps the good armies win the battle.

After the battle, Bilbo and Gandalf return to Hobbiton, where Bilbo continues to live. He is no longer accepted by respectable hobbit society, but he does not care. Bilbo now prefers to talk to elves and wizards, and he is deeply content to be back among the familiar comforts of home after his grand and harrowing adventures.

CHARACTER LIST

INDIVIDUAL CHARACTERS

Bilbo Baggins The hero of the story. Bilbo is a hobbit, "a short, human-like person." Commonsensical and fastidious, Bilbo leads a quiet life in his comfortable hole at Bag End and, like most hobbits, is content to stay at home. But Bilbo possesses a great deal of untapped inner strength, and when the wizard Gandalf persuades Bilbo to join a group of dwarves on a quest to reclaim their gold from a marauding dragon, Bilbo ends up playing a crucial role as the company's burglar. Bilbo's adventures awaken his courage and initiative and prove his relentless ability to do what needs to be done.

Gandalf A wise old wizard who always seems to know more than he reveals. Gandalf has a vast command of magic and tends to show up at just the moment he is needed most. Though he helps the dwarves in their quest (not least by making Bilbo go along with them), he does not seem to have any interest in their gold. He always has another purpose or plan in mind, but he rarely reveals his private thoughts.

Thorin Oakenshield A dwarf who leads his fellow dwarves on a trip to the Lonely Mountain to reclaim their treasure from Smaug. Smaug's bounty is Thorin's inheritance, as it belonged to Thror, Thorin's grandfather, the great King under the Mountain. Thorin is a proud, purposeful, and sturdy warrior, if a bit stubborn at times. As the novel progresses, his inability to formulate successful plans, his greed, and his reliance on Bilbo to save him at every turn make Thorin a somewhat unappealing figure, but he is partly redeemed by the remorse he shows before he dies.

Gollum   A strange, small, slimy creature who lives deep in the caves of Moria beneath the Misty Mountains. There, Gollum broods over his "precious," a magic ring, until he accidentally loses it and Bilbo finds it. We never learn exactly what kind of creature he is. Apparently, his true shape has been too deformed by years of living in darkness to be recognizable.

Smaug   The great dragon who lives in the Lonely Mountain. Years ago, Smaug heard of the treasure that the dwarves had amassed in the mountain under Thror's reign, and he drove them away to claim the gold for himself. His flaming breath can scorch a city, his huge wings can carry him great distances, and his armorlike hide is almost impenetrable. Smaug can speak and possesses a dark, sardonic sense of humor.

Bard   The grim human who is the honorable captain of the guard in Lake Town, a human city built on Long Lake just south of the Lonely Mountain. With the help of information discovered by Bilbo and related by a thrush, Bard finds Smaug's weak spot and kills him.

Beorn   A man who can turn into a bear, Beorn helps Bilbo and the dwarves after their escape from the goblins.

Elrond   The great leader of the elves at Rivendell. Elrond gives Bilbo's group aid and helpful advice when they pass through Rivendell early in the novel. He is described in Chapter 3 as being "as strong as a warrior, as wise as a wizard, as venerable as a king of dwarves, and as kind as summer."

Dark Lord Sauron   An evil sorcerer and creator of the magic ring. Also called the Necromancer, Sauron is only mentioned in *The Hobbit*; he never actually appears.

Thror   Thorin's grandfather. Thror mined Moria, a series of caves under the Mountain, and discovered a wealth of gold and jewels. He became King under the Mountain, but before long, the dragon Smaug came and killed or scattered all of Thror's people. The dragon has been guarding the treasure ever since, and Thorin wants to get back what is rightfully his.

RACES

Dwarves Thorin's group, composed of Fili, Kili, Dwalin, Balin, Oin, Gloin, Ori, Dori, Nori, Bifur, Bofur, and Bombur, none of whom is really developed as an individual character in the novel. The narrator describes dwarves unfavorably in Chapter 12, noting their greed and trickery. Some, however, are "decent enough people like Thorin and Company, if you don't expect too much."

Elves The first creatures in Middle-Earth. Immortal unless killed in battle, they are fair-faced, with beautiful voices, and have a close communion with nature, which makes them wonderful craftsmen. There are actually two different varieties of elves: the wood elves and the high elves. The wood elves reside in Mirkwood and, as a result, have more suspicious and less wise tendencies than their high relatives.

Humans Humans appear in the settlement of Lake Town near the Lonely Mountain. Tolkien emphasizes their mortality, their lack of wisdom, their discordance with nature, and their rampant feuding, but he does not describe humans as inherently evil in the same way that he characterizes goblins and Wargs.

Trolls Short-tempered and dull-witted creatures who will eat just about anything, the trolls are based on mythological creatures taken from Old English and Anglo-Saxon poems and on figures from popular fairy tales and folklore. Tolkien has them speak with a cockney accent, the dialect of lower-class Londoners, which injects a modern joke into the fantasy epic.

Goblins   Evil creatures encountered by Bilbo and company in Chapter 4. Goblins are infamous for their ability to make cruel weapons and torture devices.

Wargs   Evil wolves that join forces with the Goblins at the Battle of the Five Armies in Chapters 17 and 18. The Wargs haunt and pursue Bilbo and the dwarves soon after Bilbo acquires the ring.

ANALYSIS OF MAJOR CHARACTERS

BILBO

The protagonist and title character of *The Hobbit*, Bilbo is by far the novel's most important figure. Bilbo's thoughts, feelings, and actions form the focus of the novel and shape its plot. Bilbo's central role is underscored by his appeal—he is not only the most important but also the most likable and honorable character. Even as the other participants in his quest become corrupted by greed, Bilbo maintains his common sense, courage, and eagerness to please.

Bilbo's understated charisma is a quality common to many protagonists in children's literature. Another quality he shares with many heroes of children's literature is his small size: as a hobbit, Bilbo is only half the size of a man. At the beginning of the novel, Bilbo is, like most hobbits, comfortable and complacent. He loves food, drink, and security, and he relishes his snug little hole at Bag End, Underhill. But as Gandalf says, there is more to Bilbo than meets the eye. Bilbo is a Baggins, the heir of a thoroughly respectable and conventional family, but his mother was a Took, an eccentric clan of hobbits noted for their love of excitement and adventure.

When Gandalf enlists Bilbo's help in Thorin's quest for the treasure under the mountain, Bilbo begins a process of gradual development, transforming from a cautious homebody at the beginning of the novel to a brave and confident hero at the end. As the quest progresses, Bilbo shows a vast reserve of inner cunning and strength and slowly becomes the dominant force holding the group of hapless dwarves together. He saves them from the goblins by shouting for Gandalf, he rescues them from spiders and wood elves in Mirkwood, he finds the way into the mountain, he leads them to the treasure, he discovers Smaug's weak spot, and he attempts to thwart Thorin's greed and to bring peace to the feuding dwarves, elves, and humans.

Bilbo's heroic deeds are all the more remarkable because they fail to change him. He discovers capabilities that had been unknown to him, but he does not become arrogant or relinquish his values. In his final conversation with Bilbo, Thorin acknowledges the value of the simple lives of hobbits, even in a world marked by grim heroism and danger. Though Bilbo learns to thrive in this outer world, he draws strength from the simple source that guided his heroic quest. His decision to return to Hobbiton toward the end of the novel indicates that, despite his newfound heroism, Bilbo has stayed true to himself all along.

GANDALF

Though his history and character are more fully explored in *The Lord of the Rings* and *The Silmarillion,* Gandalf remains a looming mystery in *The Hobbit,* a constant reminder that Middle-Earth is more vast and cryptic than Bilbo realizes. A powerful wizard, Gandalf generally prefers to keep his powers and motives closely guarded. He never reveals, for instance, why he chooses to help Thorin in his quest; he certainly has no interest in the treasure, and he leaves the company in Mirkwood while he goes to fight against the Necromancer. Something both inspiring and dangerous defines Gandalf's character—he is an unshakable bulwark against evil, and yet he seems to have an enlightened, almost godlike knowledge of every person's place in the world.

Gandalf's sweeping, epic personality separates him from the vast majority of characters that commercial fantasy literature has produced in the decades since *The Hobbit* was first published. Though Gandalf can be viewed as the source of the stereotypical figure of fantasy wizard, Gandalf himself is more than just an old man with powerful spells and a pointy hat. Tolkien imbues Gandalf with a sense of heightened awareness, ensuring that Gandalf always knows more about what is happening than we do, even when the other characters are left in the dark.

THORIN

The leader of the dwarves who embark on the treasure quest in Chapter 2, Thorin is in many ways a typical member of his race: brave, stubborn, proud, and greedy for gold. Though his birthright and noble bearing initially make Thorin seem like a fairly heroic figure, the dwarf's status quickly declines as Bilbo's rises. Soon after Gandalf leaves the party, it becomes apparent that Thorin is not a true leader: he is incapable of formulating a plan, makes hasty and poor decisions, and generally relies on Bilbo to see him through his adventures, all the while treating Bilbo like an insignificant under-ling. Once Thorin gets his hands on Smaug's treasure, he becomes irrationally greedy and obsessed with wealth, to the extent that he would rather wage a violent war than give the men from Lake Town their fair share of the treasure. Thorin is partially redeemed by his dying apology to Bilbo, but not even this act of remorse can fully redeem him. In general, the arrogant Thorin works as a foil for the unassuming Bilbo, setting off Bilbo's best qualities and creating a leadership void that provides Bilbo the chance to seize the initiative and become a true hero.

CHARACTER ANALYSIS

THEMES, MOTIFS &
SYMBOLS

THEMES

Themes are the fundamental and often universal ideas explored in a literary work.

BILBO'S HEROISM
The Hobbit's main theme is Bilbo's development into a hero, which more broadly represents the development of a common person into a hero. At the beginning of the story, Bilbo is timid, comfortable, and complacent in his secure little hole at Bag End. When Gandalf talks him into embarking on the quest with Thorin's dwarves, Bilbo becomes so frightened that he faints. But as the novel progresses, Bilbo prevails in the face of danger and adversity, justifying Gandalf's early claim that there is more to the little hobbit than meets the eye.

Bilbo possesses hidden reserves of inner strength that even Bilbo himself cannot perceive when he firsts sets out on the quest. Confronting the trolls, escaping with Gollum's ring, slaying the spider, rescuing the dwarves in Mirkwood, and speaking face-to-face with the great dragon Smaug all provide Bilbo with opportunities to test his resolve. As he builds confidence and resourcefulness, Bilbo emerges as a true hero.

Because Tolkien acknowledged that the idea of hobbits was rooted in his experiences with rural Englishmen of his own time, Bilbo's development might allegorically represent the heroism of England in World War I or the inner, latent heroism common to everyone. But given Tolkien's stated distaste for allegory—his main motivation for writing was storytelling, not the exploration of a literary theme—it is questionable whether Bilbo's story should be taken to refer to anyone except Bilbo himself.

RACE, LINEAGE, AND CHARACTER
The differences among Tolkien's imaginary races are a major focus of the novel, particularly in its second half. Elves, dwarves, trolls, and goblins differ from one another physically, psychologically,

and morally. These inherent racial differences drastically limit the possibility of individual choice but make moral distinctions easy to maintain. All goblins are evil, for example, and all elves are good. The notion of races having different moral qualities is reflected in the novel's idea of nature. The good races are portrayed as being in harmony with nature, while the evil races are depicted as being at odds with it—hence the eagles' decision to help the elves against the goblins. Some critics have suggested that the different races in *The Hobbit* were meant to represent different European nationalities, but Tolkien's distaste for allegory makes this seem highly unlikely.

Family lineage is another important factor that shapes identity in *The Hobbit*. Throughout Middle-Earth, one's prospects, character, and social position are linked closely to family heritage. Bilbo's conflicting feelings of fear and courage, for instance, are portrayed as a struggle between his Baggins side and his Took side, referring respectively to his father's and his mother's families. Thorin is prompted to seek the treasure under the mountain because it is his birthright, passed down from his grandfather, Thror. Bard's heroism is in part attributed to his having descended from the lords of Dale. Whereas race is primarily a determinant of one's moral standing, family has more to do with one's specific personality: Bilbo is good because he is a hobbit, but he is adventurous because he is a Took.

MOTIFS

Motifs are recurring structures, contrasts, and literary devices that can help to develop and inform the text's major themes.

CONTRASTING WORLDVIEWS

Tolkien was a scholar of ancient languages at Oxford. A major source of inspiration for *The Hobbit*'s plot was the body of ancient epic literature that Tolkien studied, particularly Scandinavian and Anglo-Saxon epics like *Beowulf*. Elements of the story originate from literature, including the form of the heroic quest, the dragon's treasure hoard, the importance of named swords, the elves' mysterious magic, and the grim focus on birthright and family lineage.

The Hobbit revisits many of these ancient conventions with a playful, comic tone that is thoroughly modern. Bilbo himself, with his common sense, love of peace, and warmhearted self-doubt, is in many ways a rural Englishman of the 1930s transplanted into a medieval adventure. Tolkien's exploration of this contrast between the world in which he lived and the worlds he studied is the source

MOTIFS

of a large part of the book's comedy. This contrast also has some thematic importance—Thorin's last words to Bilbo indicate that despite the grandeur of epic heroism, the simple modern values of the hobbits perhaps have a more important place in the world.

THE NATURE AND GEOGRAPHY OF MIDDLE-EARTH

Since *The Hobbit* takes place in a world of the author's own creation—complete with its own history, language, geography, and mythology—much of the narrative is devoted to incidental descriptions of the places, people, and things that Bilbo encounters. As a result, Middle-Earth emerges as a finely detailed reality with a convincing visual presence and its own unique atmosphere. Taking the reader through this world is one of the primary considerations of the novel, and a great part of Tolkien's literary ingenuity is devoted to making Middle-Earth seem as real as possible. For many readers, experiencing Middle-Earth as a self-contained whole is probably the most striking aspect of reading *The Hobbit*.

SYMBOLS

Symbols are objects, characters, figures, and colors used to represent abstract ideas or concepts.

NAMED SWORDS

Throughout epic literature, swords with names and lineages are the marks of great heroes. One of the most famous examples is King Arthur's sword, Excalibur. The swords named Orcrist and Glamdring that Thorin and Gandalf win from the trolls symbolize their heroic deeds. Bilbo's decision to name his short sword Sting after killing the spider is a major turning point in his quest—it symbolizes his bravery and initiative, and presages his transformation into a hero.

HOBBITS

Though the thematic importance of hobbits is highly debatable, Tolkien himself acknowledged that the nature of hobbits was based on the rural, middle-class English people among whom he lived. This symbol enables Tolkien to explore the contrast between ancient and modern worldviews as the modern-minded Bilbo travels the ancient world of Middle-Earth.

SUMMARY & ANALYSIS

CHAPTER 1

There is a lot more in him than you guess, and a deal
more than he has any idea of himself.

(See QUOTATIONS, *p. 42)*

SUMMARY

Hobbits, the narrator explains, are little people, roughly half the
size of humans, with thick hair on their feet, round bellies, and a
love of good food, comfort, and security. Though some hobbits live
in houses, they traditionally live in holes in the ground. The holes
are not dank and smelly but comfortable, cozy underground dwell-
ings with all the amenities of their aboveground counterparts. The
hole occupied by the hobbit known as Bilbo Baggins is called Bag
End. It is quite a pleasant dwelling, with comfortable furniture and
a well-stocked kitchen, nestled in a snug little village under a hill.

Bilbo's ancestry is somewhat noble by hobbit standards: his father was from the well-to-do, conventional Baggins family, but his
mother was from the Tooks, a wealthy, eccentric family infamous for
their unhobbitlike tendency to go on adventures. Despite his Took
blood, however, Bilbo prefers to stay at home and live a quiet life.

On the day the story begins, Bilbo is enjoying a pipe outside his
front door when an old man with a long cloak and a staff arrives.
After the old man introduces himself, Bilbo recognizes him as the
wizard Gandalf, who has created spectacular fireworks displays on
holidays in Hobbiton, but Bilbo still looks on the old wizard with a
suspicious eye. When Gandalf asks if Bilbo would be interested in
going on an adventure, Bilbo declines and quickly excuses himself.
He invites the wizard to come over for tea sometime but only so as
not to seem rude—in reality, he wants nothing to do with Gandalf
and his adventures.

When the doorbell rings the next afternoon, Bilbo assumes it is
Gandalf. To his surprise, a dwarf named Dwalin pushes past him
and promptly sits down to eat. Soon, other dwarves begin to arrive, and as Bilbo's neat little home becomes crowded with dwarves,
Bilbo becomes increasingly confused and annoyed. At last, Gandalf
arrives with the head dwarf, Thorin. The thirteen dwarves and the

wizard nearly clean out Bilbo's pantry before finally settling down to discuss their business.

It soon becomes clear that Gandalf has volunteered Bilbo to be a "burglar" for the dwarves on their adventure. The hobbit protests, and the dwarves grumble that the soft little hobbit does not seem suited to their adventure. Gandalf, however, is certain that Bilbo is useful, and insists that there is more to the hobbit than meets the eye.

The wizard then brings out an old map of a great mountain and points to a mysterious secret entrance, a door to which Thorin holds the key. Bilbo demands some clarification about the point of the whole expedition. Thorin explains that his grandfather, Thror, mined the mountain shown on the map and discovered a wealth of gold and jewels. Thror then became King under the Mountain, but his fantastic treasure attracted unwanted attention. Before long, the dragon Smaug came and killed or scattered all of Thror's people. The dragon has been guarding the treasure ever since. Thorin and the dwarves are out to reclaim their rightful inheritance, even though they are unsure of what to do with Smaug when they find him.

Bilbo suspects that the dwarves want him to play a part in slaying the dragon. Although his Baggins side would like nothing better than to sit at home with his pipe, the Took influence in him fuels his curiosity about the adventure, and he is reluctantly excited by the tales of dragons and treasure and great battles. After looking at the map and discussing the adventure with the company, the hobbit makes up beds for all his guests and then spends the night in troubled dreams.

ANALYSIS

In *The Hobbit*, Tolkien presents us with a fantasy world of his own creation, complete with its own races, languages, and geography. Tolkien was a language scholar, and he was partially motivated to write his stories by his desire to invent other languages. He implies at the beginning of Chapter 1 that this fantasy world, which he later dubbed Middle-Earth, is somehow connected to our own world, saying that hobbits "have become rare and shy of the Big People," which is why we no longer see them around.

In *The Silmarillion* and *The Lord of the Rings,* Tolkien implies that Middle-Earth is our Earth as it existed millions of years ago, when the continents had very different forms. Thus, Tolkien's world is as much mythological as it is fantastic. Its larger purpose, like that of Greek and Roman mythologies, is often to reflect truths about our own world that may be better seen when presented in a mythical context. In fact, Tolkien first wrote about Middle-Earth with the intention of creating an entirely new mythology for the English people, and the story's form is based on the ancient heroic epics that Tolkien taught and studied at Oxford. But *The Hobbit* is only tangentially connected to Tolkien's history of Middle-Earth and to the larger mythology that Tolkien would explore in his longer and more ambitious works.

The Hobbit's tone is much warmer and more humorous than that of most heroic epics, such as *Beowulf*. Tolkien tested out *The Hobbit* as he wrote it by reading it to his sons, and the manner of narration is, at times, very much like a children's story. Its style is extremely playful and conversational, with frequent asides and jokes directed at the audience, including one famous quip about how an ancestor of the Tooks invented the game of golf when a goblin's head he had chopped off in battle rolled into a hole.

The unlikely pairing of Bilbo with wizards, dwarves, and dragons in the first chapter establishes the contrast between the novel's historically inspired, mythological subject matter and its lighthearted, modern tone. Much of the humor in the novel's early chapters stems from this contrast. For example, as the dwarves hold their great feast, Bilbo worries that they will chip his plates and furniture—both Bilbo and the dwarves end up looking slightly ridiculous. The hobbit's skeptical outlook on his guests and on the adventure mirrors our own outlook, and it enables the story's more fantastic elements to be introduced in a manner that is more entertaining than explanatory. Tolkien eases us into his fantasy world, so that as Bilbo develops into a bolder and more heroic figure, we also become more familiar with the magical landscape of Middle-Earth.

In the preface to *The Lord of the Rings,* Tolkien conveyed his distaste for allegory. In the decades after writing *The Hobbit,* however, he openly acknowledged the link between hobbits and the English people of his own time. There are even many similarities between Bilbo and Tolkien. Like Bilbo, Tolkien enjoyed middle-class comforts—simple food, a pipe, and a quiet life. Like Bilbo, Tolkien had "adventurous blood"—his mother was from a family known for its extensive escapades. In a more general sense, Bilbo can be seen as a gentle caricature of the English—a reserved, quiet people who, nevertheless, can be roused to action when the situation calls for it, a trait Tolkien witnessed firsthand during his service in World War I.

CHAPTERS 2–3

SUMMARY: CHAPTER 2

Bilbo wakes up rather late the morning after Gandalf's visit. He is surprised—and a little relieved—to see that the dwarves have left without him. He is just sitting down to a quiet breakfast when Gandalf enters and rushes him off to the Green Dragon Inn, in Bywater, where Thorin and the rest of the dwarves have been waiting to begin their journey. As they head east on the main road, Bilbo sulks at having to leave without finishing his second breakfast or making proper preparations. It begins to rain. By the time dusk approaches, the whole company is tired, hungry, ready to camp, and annoyed at Gandalf's mysterious disappearance earlier in the day.

Suddenly they see what looks like the light of a fire in the distance. They move closer to investigate it, and Bilbo is sent ahead in his first official task as burglar. As he approaches a clearing in the woods, Bilbo sees three huge trolls sitting around a fire, eating mutton. Bilbo tries to make off with one of the trolls' money purses, but they hear the noise and grab him. Trolls will eat just about anything, but they are also short-tempered and dull-witted. They proceed to fight about how to interrogate Bilbo.

The commotion attracts the dwarves, who come to the clearing one at a time. The trolls stop fighting just long enough to hide in the trees and throw a sack over each approaching dwarf. Soon, they have everyone tied up except Bilbo, whom they've forgotten. The trolls decide to cook the dwarves immediately, but then a voice, which sounds like one of the trolls, starts an argument, and the three trolls start fighting again. This fighting goes on for quite some time until the trolls notice that it is almost dawn. The sun peeks over the horizon and the trolls all freeze—sunlight turns trolls to stone.

Gandalf then steps triumphantly into the clearing. He had been throwing his voice to mislead the dwarves and to keep the trolls arguing until morning. He and Bilbo release the dwarves, who are shaken but otherwise unharmed. Searching nearby, they find the trolls' cave and a number of well-wrought weapons, which they take as payment for their pains.

SUMMARY: CHAPTER 3

As the company sets off the next morning, Gandalf explains that he has checked the road ahead up to the last safe stop along their way. This stop is Rivendell, a city of elves located just beyond the Edge of the Wild, near the foothills of the Misty Mountains, which the company will have to pass. As the company approaches Rivendell, a number of elves approach them and invite them back to eat and rest. During their stay, they meet Elrond, the great chief elf, who is "as strong as a warrior, as wise as a wizard, as venerable as a king of dwarves, and as kind as summer."

Elrond can interpret the ancient runes, or markings, found on the company's new weapons and on Thorin's map of the mountain. The swords taken from the trolls, he tells them, are renowned goblin-killers from the great wars between the elves and the goblins. Gandalf's sword is called Glamdring, and Thorin's is named Orcist. On Thorin's map, Elrond is able to read moon-letters—writing visible only in the light of the moon in the proper phase—that describe how to find the secret entrance on the Lonely Mountain. Though they are puzzled by the message, the group is in high spirits when they depart from Rivendell. Everyone is well rested and prepared for the road ahead.

ANALYSIS: CHAPTERS 2–3

Bilbo's impulsive bravery in the troll camp—including his burglar-like attempt to steal a money purse—begins his figurative transformation from an introvert to an adventurer. Though Bilbo is relieved when he thinks the dwarves have gone on without him, by the end of Chapter 2, he has already begun to prove Gandalf's claim that there is more to Bilbo than meets the eye. Over the course of the novel, Bilbo gradually sheds his modern complacency and becomes more courageous and adventurous.

In the characters of the trolls, Tolkien combines characteristics of mythological creatures taken from Old English and Anglo-Saxon poems with those of popular fairy tales and folklore. The dwarves' one-by-one approach to the troll camp subtly alludes to the sequential narratives of children's fables like "The Three Billy-Goats Gruff," which also features a group's one-by-one confrontation with a troll. Tolkien also injects some modern humor into the story by giving the trolls cockney accents, the dialect of lower-class Londoners: "Mutton yesterday, mutton today, and blimey, if it don't look like mutton again tomorrer."

The swords that the company steals from the trolls' cave are a link to the tradition of heroic epic on which so many aspects of *The Hobbit* are based. Great swords that have mythic lineages and heroic names are characteristically present in heroic epics, the most famous example being King Arthur's legendary sword, Excalibur. The possession of a named sword is a symbol of heroism and prowess in battle, and for this reason, it is significant that Bilbo's short sword is *not* named yet. As we shall see, after Bilbo performs some deeds more worthy of his quest, he names his sword.

In *The Silmarillion,* the swords are described as having been made for the goblin wars of an earlier age of Middle-Earth, in which the elves fought off the goblins. There is no question of which side was good and which evil—the evil nature of the goblins is described in Chapter 4, and the good nature of the elves is obvious from the glimpse we get of them at Rivendell in Chapter 3. Elves were the first creatures in Middle-Earth: they are immortal unless killed in battle; they are fair-faced, with beautiful voices; and they have a close communion with nature, which makes them skillful craftsmen. The unique magic of the swords, as Elrond tells the company in Chapter 3, is that they glow with a blue light when goblins are near.

CHAPTERS 4–5

SUMMARY: CHAPTER 4

Bilbo and company advance upon the Misty Mountains. Thanks to Elrond's and Gandalf's advice, they are able to find a good pass over the mountain range among the many dead-end trails and drop-offs. Still, the climb is long and treacherous. A violent thunderstorm breaks suddenly, forcing them to find shelter. Luckily, two of the dwarves (Fili and Kili) find a cave in a side of the mountain. They bring in the ponies and make camp for the night.

In the middle of the night, Bilbo wakes with a start, just in time to see the ponies get dragged into an enormous crack that has opened in the cave wall. He yells, and out of the crack jump dozens of goblins, who tie up and carry off each member of the company except Gandalf, who was forewarned by Bilbo's yell.

The goblins carry the dwarves and the hobbit down into the mountain to a huge chamber where the Great Goblin sits. He demands to know what the travelers are doing in his mountain. Thorin tries to explain about the storm, but one of the goblins brings forth the sword that Thorin took from the trolls, which he was carrying when captured. This sword, Orcrist, the goblin-cleaver, is well-known among the goblins.

The goblins go into a rage and the Great Goblin lunges at Thorin to eat him. Suddenly, the torches lighting the cavern go out and the great fire in the middle of the chamber throws its sparks onto the goblins. In the darkness and confusion, a great sword flashes and strikes down the Great Goblin. Then a voice guides the captives out of the cavern. It is Gandalf, who leads the dwarves through the passages and deeper into the mountain. The goblins follow quickly after them, and one of the goblins catches up to the dwarf Dori, who has been carrying Bilbo on his back. Bilbo falls off, strikes his head on the ground, and loses consciousness.

SUMMARY: CHAPTER 5

> It's got to ask uss a question, my preciouss, yes, yess,
> yess. Jusst one more question to guess, yes, yess.
> (See QUOTATIONS, p. 42)

When Bilbo regains consciousness, he can see nothing in the darkness. Feeling around on the floor, he happens to come across a ring, which he puts in his pocket. He has no idea where the rest of the company is, or in which direction the exit lies. Picking the path he feels he had been traveling with the dwarves, he soon comes across an underground lake. There, he discovers a strange creature named Gollum. When Gollum sees Bilbo prowling around, obviously lost, he is interested and a bit hungry, so he approaches the hobbit. Bilbo brandishes his sword when he hears Gollum's hissing voice.

Gollum does not wish to contend with the sword, so he proposes a riddle game. If Gollum's riddle stumps Bilbo, he will eat Bilbo, but if Bilbo's stumps Gollum, Gollum will show Bilbo the way out of the mountain. Bilbo has no choice but to agree, and they begin asking each other riddles. In the end, Bilbo wins through a bit of trickery. Referring to the ring he had found, he asks, "What have I got in my pocket?" and Gollum cannot guess the right answer. Gollum, however, does not intend to let his meal get away so easily. He goes to his island in the middle of the lake to get his "precious," a golden ring that makes its wearer invisible—the very ring that Bilbo had found.

Unable to find the ring, Gollum suspects the hobbit of stealing it and runs at him in a rage. Through sheer luck, Bilbo happens to slip on the ring, and Gollum runs right past him. Realizing the ring's power, Bilbo follows Gollum, who heads toward the exit thinking that Bilbo is ahead of him. When Gollum gets near the exit, he stops because there are goblins crowded around it. Bilbo leaps over him, runs past the goblins unnoticed thanks to the ring, and just barely manages to squeeze through the door into freedom and fresh air.

ANALYSIS: CHAPTERS 4–5

The uniform wickedness demonstrated by the goblins in Chapter 4 affirms the connection between race and moral tendencies in Tolkien's fantasy world. The different races of Middle-Earth possess specific moral characteristics, so that goblins, who are infamous for their ability to make cruel weapons and instruments of torture, are evil, and elves are good. There are no exceptions. The races of Middle-Earth also possess qualities that have little direct bearing on their overall moral standing. Hobbits love food, for instance, and dwarves love gold. Again, there are no exceptions.

The characteristics of the races result primarily from the mythic theology of Middle-Earth. Under this theology, the gods create certain creatures for very specific purposes. Each race also has a particular relationship with nature. Of the various characters Tolkien depicts, Bilbo seems to be the only one capable of making complex moral choices that test the boundaries of his race.

Bilbo's heroism is somewhat dubious, for though he behaves heroically, his acts seem to be the result of luck, or else destiny, rather than effort on his part. He seems to have a knack for being in the right place at the right time. In his first encounter with the goblins, for example, Bilbo proves useful by shouting enough to awaken Gandalf, who, in turn, ends up saving the whole company. Bilbo is credited for helping the whole party when his companions were unable to do so, even though it was only his chance awakening that enabled him to warn everyone.

Bilbo's unintentional heroism is most evident in his discovery of the magic ring. In the history of Middle-Earth, this discovery is the most important event in the novel. Though neither Bilbo nor Gollum (the ring's previous holder) are aware of it, the ring is in fact an object of awesome power. Created by the Dark Lord Sauron, who appears in *The Hobbit* as the Necromancer of Mirkwood, the ring is central to Sauron's attempt to conquer and corrupt the world. The ring is pivotal to the plot of *The Lord of the Rings*. In *The Hobbit,* its greater importance is only hinted at when Tolkien cryptically comments that Bilbo's discovery of the ring is a turning point in his career.

Gollum's whiny, hissing style of speech marks him as one of the novel's most unique and memorable characters. Gollum's riddle game is itself another example of Tolkien's interaction with epic literature in *The Hobbit*. Riddles and riddle games are familiar features of Anglo-Saxon and Scandinavian epics, in which heroes are defined almost as much by their prowess with words as they are by their prowess with swords. In fact, many of the riddles exchanged by Bilbo and Gollum come directly from ancient Scandinavian and Anglo-Saxon poems. Bilbo's victory in the riddle game is an important step in his development, but the eccentric manner in which he wins is closer to that of modern comedy than to that of ancient epic. Bilbo baffles Gollum with the question, "What have I got in my pocket?," which is, of course, not a true riddle at all. A true riddle must contain clues necessary to solve it. Gollum, with his purely ancient sensibilities, cannot even challenge Bilbo's question, let alone answer it.

CHAPTERS 6–7

SUMMARY: CHAPTER 6

Fleeing from the goblins—and still invisible, thanks to the ring—Bilbo looks back and realizes that he has made it to the other side of the Misty Mountains. The tunnels have taken him all the way through the range. Walking along, he stumbles upon Gandalf and the dwarves, who have just been wondering whether they should leave without him. The hobbit slips off the ring and surprises them and then explains how he made his way out of the mountain. However, he refrains from mentioning his discovery of the magic ring and the role it played in his escape from Gollum and the goblins.

Gandalf implores the company to get moving again since only the sunlight is keeping the goblins from coming after them. The group is a bit north of where they had planned to be, and they have difficult country to cross. Evening comes as they pass through a grove of trees. Suddenly, they hear the howling of wolves and barely have time to scurry up into the trees before the wolves descend upon them. The beasts are actually wolflike creatures called Wargs. The Wargs are allies of the goblins, and they quickly notify the goblins of the situation. The goblins begin to arrive and, laughing at the company's predicament, light fires under the trees in which Gandalf, the dwarves, and Bilbo are hiding.

Gandalf prepares to attack the goblins, hoping to kill as many as he can before they kill him. Luckily for the company, the Lord of the Eagles has seen the commotion from his roost high in the mountains. With a number of other eagles, he swoops down, picks up the marooned travelers, and flies them to safety. The eagles are friends of Gandalf's and enemies of the goblins. They are happy to provide food and rest for the weary travelers, who then continue on their journey.

Summary: Chapter 7

Once again, Gandalf disappoints the company by announcing that he must leave. He says, however, that he will stay around long enough to help them find food and ponies so that they can make their way on their own through Mirkwood—the last great obstacle before the Lonely Mountain. He leads them to the house of Beorn. Beorn is a half-man, half-bear creature who has a great wooden house in the middle of the woods outside Mirkwood. Gandalf takes the dwarves to Beorn's house a few at a time, so as not to startle him. He tells Beorn the story of their adventure in the mountain. Gandalf's story amuses Beorn greatly because he despises goblins, who are enemies of nature.

Beorn offers the company much-needed food and lodging. He also does some scouting and finds that the Wargs and goblins have put together an attack party in order to find the dwarves and wizard that killed their leader, the Great Goblin. To evade this attack party, Beorn recommends that the group take the northern pass (the elf path) through Mirkwood, which will bring them near the Lonely Mountain. This choice will throw the goblins off the company's trail and allow them to bypass the dangerous southern pass. The northern pass is not entirely safe either, so Beorn repeatedly warns his guests never to stray from the path.

Beorn provides the group with food and ponies to carry them to the gate at the path's start. From there, however, they must return the ponies and travel on foot. When they reach the path, Gandalf also departs, wishing his friends the best and reminding them never to stray from the path—dark things lurk in Mirkwood that even the wizard does not know about. On that note, the dwarves and the hobbit plunge into the forest.

Analysis: Chapters 6–7

Although the eagles and Beorn help the company tremendously, they both express that hatred for goblins, rather than love for dwarves, is their main reason for helping the company. Neither Beorn nor the eagles have any interest in the dwarves' gold, but as representatives of pure nature, they are the sworn enemies of corrupted nature, represented by the goblins and Wargs. The eagles generally keep distant from the affairs of other races, and Beorn can be downright cruel to those who displease him. When he finds a goblin and a Warg prowling about in the woods, for instance, he puts the goblin's head on a stake and the Warg's pelt on a tree outside his house as a warning. Beorn and the eagles show all the brute force of nature and, in fact, seem to be part of it. Gandalf surmises that, long ago, Beorn was born from the mountains themselves.

By the end of Chapter 7, the episodic nature of *The Hobbit* narrative becomes increasingly clear. Like successive episodes of a popular television show, each chapter brings a new setting and a new set of adventures. Chapter 2 involved the trolls, Chapter 3 introduced us to Elrond and Rivendell, Chapter 4 involved the goblins, Chapter 5 chronicled Bilbo's encounter with Gollum, and so forth. Once an adventure is completed, it generally has relatively little bearing on the rest of the novel. The one continuous thread, however, is that the changes Bilbo undergoes as a result of each adventure affect his behavior in subsequent adventures.

Moreover, until the group nears its destination at the Lonely Mountain, the particular adventures that they face have little to do with their ultimate goal of regaining Thorin's treasure. Dangers like the goblins and the tempest are merely incidental obstacles the characters encounter on the way to their destination. These impediments make up *The Hobbit*'s cast of antagonists, each of whom predominates in a single adventure. Examples of particular antagonists include the Great Goblin, the spiders of Mirkwood, and the great dragon Smaug.

The novel's overall tone grows darker and more ominous the farther the company travels, so that the solace they find in Beorn's lair after escaping the goblins seems grim and violent compared to the solace they found in Rivendell after escaping the trolls. Even after the company escapes the goblins, the coming journey into Mirkwood seems so perilous that the road ahead seems more frightening than the road behind. This gradually darkening tone builds tension. It also transforms the novel's dynamic from a lighthearted children's story into a more serious epic. This gradual change corresponds to the reader's immersion into the tale and to Bilbo's transformation into a true hero. As Bilbo travels farther from the safe and familiar comforts of Hobbiton, the dangers he faces heighten, and he evolves from a humble hobbit into a noble protagonist heroically negotiating his way through evil.

CHAPTERS 8–9

SUMMARY: CHAPTER 8

> *Somehow [after] the killing of this giant spider ... [h]e*
> *felt a different person, and much fiercer and bolder in*
> *spite of an empty stomach, as he wiped his sword on*
> *the grass and put it back into its sheath.*
>
> (See QUOTATIONS, p. 43)

Darkness falls upon Bilbo and the dwarves as they enter the bleak forest of Mirkwood. Strange eyes peer out at them from the trees. Soon, the group cannot tell night from day. Everyone can think only of getting out of the stuffy, ominous woods, but there seems to be no end in sight. After a few days, they come to a stream that Beorn had warned them not to touch. They cross using a boat already moored there, but a dwarf, Bombur, falls in and is put into a sleep that lasts for days. The rest of the party is forced to carry him. Hungry, tired, and scared, they begin to despair.

One night, they see a flicker of lights in the trees and, ignoring the warnings of Beorn and Gandalf, they leave the path and move toward the lights. They see elves sitting in a clearing around a fire, feasting and singing. However, the moment they burst into the clearing, the lights are snuffed out, and the dwarves and Bilbo can hardly find one another. The same thing happens twice more. On the last occasion, everyone becomes separated, unable to find one another in the darkness. Soon, Bilbo stops hearing voices and, exhausted, leans against a tree to sleep.

When Bilbo awakens, his legs are bound with sticky thread and an enormous spider is advancing toward him. Whipping out his sword, he slashes his legs free and slays the spider. Flush with victory, he gives his sword a name: Sting. He then goes in search of the dwarves. To his horror, he finds them all hanging from a tree, tied up in the webs of the many spiders that sit atop the branches. Bilbo whips a few stones at the spiders and then leads them away from the dwarves by yelling. Fortunately, he is wearing the ring all the while, so the spiders cannot find him.

Having led the spiders away, Bilbo slips back and cuts the dwarves free. But the spiders soon return, and the dwarves, weak from the spiders' poison, can hardly fight them off, even with the aid of the invisible Bilbo. Just when the situation looks completely hopeless, the spiders suddenly retreat, and the company realizes that they themselves have retreated into one of the clearings used by elves. There, they rest to ponder their next course of action. A moment later, they realize with horror that Thorin is missing.

Unbeknownst to the others, Thorin was taken prisoner by the elves when he stepped into the clearing before the spider attack. The elves are wood elves, who are good but suspicious of strangers. The Elvenking questions Thorin about his journey. When Thorin refuses to say where the company is going, the elves throw him in the dungeon, but they feed him and are not cruel.

SUMMARY: CHAPTER 9

Soon after Bilbo and the rest of the dwarves escape the spiders, they are surrounded by a company of wood elves and brought blindfolded to the Elvenking's halls. Bilbo, still wearing his ring, remains undetected. The other dwarves are brought before the king and questioned. Like Thorin, they refuse to reveal their plan to reclaim the treasure from Smaug for fear that the elves will demand a share. Also like Thorin, the dwarves are thrown into the dungeon. Meanwhile, Bilbo, having followed the captured dwarves, walks invisibly through the halls, whispering to the dwarves in their cells and plotting an escape.

The elves exchange goods with the men of Lake Town via barrels that are floated on a river that flows under the elves' dwelling. Empty barrels are sent floating back down the river from a storeroom. In the storeroom, Bilbo catches a guardsman napping. He steals the guardsman's keys, frees the dwarves, and puts his plan into action. He helps pack each dwarf into an empty barrel just before the elves return and shove the barrels into the river; then, still invisible, he hops onto an empty barrel. The trapdoors open and the dwarves speed out along the river toward Lake Town.

ANALYSIS: CHAPTERS 8–9

A key turning point in Bilbo's development comes when he kills the spider that wrapped him in its web as he slept. After killing the spider, Bilbo feels like "a different person." The spider is the first enemy that Bilbo defeats in combat, and the incident serves as a rite of passage. This change is marked by Bilbo's decision to name his sword. In ancient epic literature, named swords are important symbols of courage and heroism, so by giving his sword a name, Bilbo signifies his new capacity to lead and succeed. From this point on, Bilbo begins to take action and make plans on his own—his plan to free the dwarves from the wood elves is the first instance of his newfound resolve. The peril and enmity that Bilbo and his group encounter in Mirkwood, combined with Gandalf's absence and the dwarves' bad luck, provide Bilbo with a grand opportunity to continue his development into a hero.

The narrator's description of the wood elves as "Good People" who have become less wise, more suspicious, and more dangerous than the high elves, their relatives, illustrates how race and moral condition are closely linked in Tolkien's Middle-Earth. We have not yet encountered any humans in *The Hobbit,* so it is still difficult to figure where humans fit within Tolkien's hierarchy of good and evil. From the passing references that we do hear, we get the impression that humans are mortal, often unwise, out of accord with nature, and prone to feuding. Still, humans do not seem to be uniformly evil like the goblins and the Wargs. Soon, at the end of Chapter 9, we encounter more substantial evidence of man when the company, waterlogged but alive, floats toward the human settlement Lake Town, just south of the Lonely Mountain, which is the group's ultimate destination.

An evil aura pervades the forest of Mirkwood. As Gandalf explains, the evil atmosphere stems mostly from the presence of the mysterious Necromancer in the south of Mirkwood. The Necromancer does not figure in *The Hobbit* in a significant way but provides another important link between this novel and *The Lord of the Rings.* The Necromancer later proves to be Sauron, the Dark Lord, who is rebuilding his evil power in Mirkwood before returning to his stronghold of Barad-Dur in the blighted land of Mordor.

CHAPTERS 10–11

SUMMARY: CHAPTER 10

The barrels, with one hobbit on top and thirteen dwarves inside, flow down the river and out of Mirkwood forest. Looking to the north, Bilbo sees the Lonely Mountain, the group's ultimate destination. For the time being, however, the river takes them toward Lake Town (its alternate name, Esgaroth, is mentioned in Chapter 12). Lake Town is a human city, built on Long Lake, south of the Lonely Mountain. At Lake Town, the barrels are brought to shore when boats from the town row out and cast ropes toward the floaters, and while the men are away, Bilbo frees his companions from the barrels. Everyone has survived, but they are cramped, wet, and hungry.

Thorin, filled with a new sense of purpose, strides proudly up to the town hall and declares to the Master of Lake Town that he, a descendant of the King under the Mountain, has returned to claim his inheritance. The people of the town rejoice. They have all heard the stories of how gold flowed down the river when the King under the Mountain reigned before Smaug came. They treat the dwarves and even Bilbo like kings. After a fortnight, the company is strong and eager again. Though they still have no idea how to deal with the dragon, Thorin feels that they cannot wait any longer. He obtains boats, horses, and provisions from the Master of Lake Town, and the company sets off up the River running toward the Lonely Mountain.

SUMMARY: CHAPTER 11

As they approach the foothills of the Lonely Mountain, the land turns bleak and barren. All greenery and other living foliage have been burnt away by Smaug. When they reach the foot of the mountain, Bilbo and three dwarves are sent to investigate the main entrance on the south side. The entrance looks far too dangerous—it is the gate that Smaug uses—so the company decides to search out the secret door described on their map, which is on the west side of the mountain.

After hours of searching, Bilbo finally locates a narrow passage along a cliff that leads to a flat, smooth patch on the mountain's side. Though the patch must be the door, the dwarves cannot find a way to open it, as they have forgotten the message that Elrond read from the map. The dwarves bang at the door with picks and axes but to no avail. They grow discouraged.

One evening, Bilbo is sitting outside the door, lost in thought, when a thrush lands nearby and begins to knock a snail against a stone with its beak. Suddenly, the hobbit remembers the riddle on the map. He quickly gathers the other dwarves by the door, and they watch as the sun slowly sets. With the sun's last light, a single ray falls on a part of the door, and there a rock falls away to reveal a keyhole. Thorin quickly takes the key that came with the map and places it in the rock—when he turns it, the door's outlines appear. The dwarves and the hobbit push open the door and stare into the depths of the mountain before them.

ANALYSIS: CHAPTERS 10–11

The way in which Thorin Oakenshield's name and the name of his grandfather command immediate respect in Lake Town despite Thorin's tattered appearance highlights the importance of ancestry and family name in Middle-Earth. We have already seen the importance of lineage in defining a person's character and prospects, first through Bilbo's oscillation between his Took side and his Baggins side, and also through Thorin's obsession with his birthright, the treasure under the mountain. When the party arrives at Lake Town, we see that lineage also influences social interactions. Since strangers often bring trouble, a well-known name is powerful. A mark of social and familial stability, a name like Oakenshield represents a time when peace and prosperity prevailed. For the people of Lake Town, the return of the grandson of the King under the Mountain recalls a time before Smaug when gold came from the Lonely Mountain.

The introduction of the people of Lake Town places humans in Tolkien's hierarchy of good and evil races. The human denizens of Lake Town are quite cautious when it comes to confronting the dragon. When the company sets off for the mountain, the humans refuse to go near it, leaving Bilbo and the dwarves to fend for themselves. Though they are concerned most about themselves, the people of Lake Town cannot really be blamed for fearing Smaug—they are convinced that he is invincible. Though Tolkien here emphasizes human fallibility and fear, he portrays humans as generally good creatures.

With the riddle of the secret door, Tolkien draws his readers into the story by presenting a confusing puzzle that we attempt to solve before the characters do. Tolkien employs this device often—we have already seen it in the riddle game between Bilbo and Gollum. At the mountain, we have an even greater advantage over the characters. The company has passed through many dangers since their last night in Rivendell, where Elrond interpreted the moon runes on the map for them, explaining that the door could open only on Durin's Day, one of the last days of autumn. Except for Bilbo, they have quite forgotten the message about "when the thrush knocks. . . ."

We are more likely to have the message fresh in mind, however, especially since the narrator notes several times in Chapter 11 that "Autumn was now crawling towards winter." The difference between the reader's knowledge and the characters' ignorance, a situation of dramatic irony, adds to the suspense and urgency of the moment Bilbo figures out the secret of the door. Tolkien builds tension toward the descent into the mountain and the characters' confrontation with Smaug by playing upon our desire for the characters to realize what we already know.

CHAPTERS 12–13

SUMMARY: CHAPTER 12

> [D]warves are not heroes, but calculating folk with a
> great idea of the value of money; some are tricky and
> treacherous and pretty bad lots; some are not, but are
> decent enough people like Thorin and Company, if you
> don't expect too much.
>
> (See QUOTATIONS, p. 43)

The dark passage into the mountain stands open before the company. Thorin nominates Bilbo, the official burglar, to go inside to snoop. Bilbo enters, slips on his ring to make himself invisible, and proceeds down the long, dark passage into Smaug's lair. There, he sees the magnificent, terrible dragon asleep on piles of treasure. Smaug is red and gold, with fiery breath, sharp claws, and a hide as strong as a diamond. Bilbo is horribly afraid, but he works up the nerve to take a single golden cup from one of the piles. He then rushes back up to the dwarves, who marvel over the cup.

Bilbo's theft does not go unnoticed by Smaug, who takes careful account of his treasure. When he awakens, he is enraged to discover that the cup is missing. He flies around the mountain breathing blasts of flame, and when he sees the company's ponies at the foot of the mountain, he chases the ponies down and devours them. Meanwhile, the dwarves and Bilbo huddle inside the secret passage, terrified. After a while, Smaug returns to his den and falls asleep. The hobbit works up the nerve to return to the dragon's lair, only to discover that the dragon has been feigning sleep. The terrible creature is wide awake, and Smaug is waiting for Bilbo.

Although he cannot see Bilbo because of the ring, Smaug smells Bilbo and greets him mockingly. Bilbo is smart, though, and answers Smaug only in riddles, which amuses the dragon enough to quell his anger for a while. Cleverly, the hobbit flatters Smaug into displaying his thick-skinned underbelly, revealing an open patch in Smaug's scaly armor above his left breast.

Bilbo rushes back up the passage, just outrunning the dragon's angry flames. The hobbit tells the dwarves all that he has learned while a thrush sits nearby and seems to listen. They then hear the roar of the dragon once more and shut the door to the passage just before an avalanche comes down upon it. They are trapped inside the mountain.

SUMMARY: CHAPTER 13

Smaug guesses from Bilbo's riddles that the company is somehow involved with the men of Lake Town, so he flies there to wreak vengeance. The hobbit and dwarves cower in the dark passage until they can bear it no longer. They slowly creep down toward Smaug's chamber. When Bilbo determines that the beast is gone, the dwarves run out to the treasure in glee, remembering the prosperous times of old. Bilbo takes only a few things. One of them is the Arkenstone, an incomparable gem that Thorin seeks but which the hobbit decides to keep for himself. Bilbo also finds a marvelous coat of mail made of mithril, a wonderfully strong, light metal that is scarcer and more valuable than silver or gold.

After the excitement has died down, Thorin leads the company through the passages of the mountain and out the main gate at the source of the River Running. They still have no idea what to do about Smaug when he returns. In the meantime, they are desperately hungry, so they follow the river down from the mountain to an old guard-post cavern that has not been used since the days of Thror, Thorin's grandfather. There, they rest, eat, and wonder where the dragon has gone.

ANALYSIS: CHAPTERS 12–13

As the dwarves get closer to their long-lost treasure, they become more stubborn (as when they refuse to talk to the Elvenking), and they make poorer decisions (as when they leave the path in Mirkwood). They have come to rely almost entirely on Bilbo for common sense and for salvation from the results of their own blunders, and the dwarves' increasingly hardhearted haplessness gives Bilbo no choice but to further develop his newfound qualities of initiative, courage, and heroism. Bilbo is concerned about the next step of the quest, but all he can do is get the greedy dwarves away from the gold in Smaug's chambers so they can look for a safer place to rest. His frustration with the dwarves' stubborn recklessness prompts Bilbo to take and conceal the Arkenstone, the gem that Thorin covets.

Although Bilbo's motives for taking the Arkenstone are unclear, the narrator explains the dwarves' eagerness to plunder by telling us that the one love of all dwarves is money. Whether dwarves are good or bad, one cannot expect much more from them. This is not exactly glowing praise, and as the tale progresses and the dwarves' greed leads them to increasingly arrogant and foolish behavior, we are inclined to feel even less sympathy for dwarves and even more sympathy for Bilbo. The treasure fills Thorin, in particular, with pride and stubbornness, but despite his lofty rhetoric, he fails to offer any practical plan for dealing with the dragon. Like the other dwarves, he leaves this problem entirely to Bilbo while continuing to act like the party's unquestioned leader.

Smaug's character fuses elements from ancient epic literature with far more modern traits. Smaug has all the characteristics of legendary dragons, including an armorlike scaled hide, a love of treasure, and the ability to breathe fire. However, he also possesses a dark sense of humor that is thoroughly modern and an almost magical gift of speech that allows him to glean more information from Bilbo than the clever hobbit intends to give. His speech is so persuasive that he even makes Bilbo doubt, briefly, whether the dwarves are actually going to give him his share of the profits. This doubt may also play a role in Bilbo's decision to keep the Arkenstone.

In Chapter 13, Thorin's explanation for the thrush's interest in Bilbo's information about Smaug's weak spot is not idle talk. Thorin says that certain birds in the area were once used as messengers because of their peculiar ability to communicate with certain men. Thorin's comment foreshadows the dramatic events of the next chapter, in which Bilbo wins over the dragon in a battle of wits. Once again, Gandalf is proven wise for having foreseen that a simple hobbit could succeed using cleverness whereas a mighty warrior would have likely failed using might.

Chapters 14–15

Summary: Chapter 14

The narrator suspends telling the story of Bilbo and the dwarves at the mountain and focuses on Smaug as the dragon flies toward Lake Town to wreak vengeance. The people of Lake Town see the dragon coming from a long way off (some think at first that his fire is the river running with gold) and prepare archers and many buckets of water to douse the coming flames. Their readiness is of little help, for Smaug flies over the town and lights every roof on fire. The men's arrows bounce harmlessly off the dragon's diamondlike hide. When most of the men have abandoned the city, one man, Bard, the captain of the archers, readies his last arrow. Suddenly, a thrush lands on his shoulder and speaks in a language he can understand. The bird tells Bard to watch for the dragon's weak spot in the hollow of his left breast. Bard looks, sees the open patch, and lets fly his arrow. It plunges through the chink in the dragon's armor and buries itself in his heart. The beast comes crashing down, destroying the rest of Lake Town as he dies. Bard manages to dive safely into the water and join the rest of his people, who are mourning the dead and their lost town. Some blame the dwarves for waking the dragon, but most assume that they too are dead. Then the lake men remember the gold in the Lonely Mountain, and they think eagerly of how the wealth could rebuild their town.

News of Smaug's death spreads quickly. It reaches far and wide, bringing the Elvenking and an army of elves, who stop at Lake Town to lend aid. The humans and elves then gather together in a single army and march toward the Lonely Mountain. Most of them expect to find a massive treasure left unattended.

SUMMARY: CHAPTER 15
Meanwhile, the thrush returns to the company on the mountain. Finding that they cannot understand its speech, the thrush brings an old raven that can speak in the common tongue. This bird informs Bilbo and the dwarves of Smaug's death, and they rejoice. However, their rejoicing is short-lived, as the raven goes on to describe the huge army of humans and elves marching toward them, as well as the suffering of Lake Town's people, who surely deserve some share of the massive treasure in the mountain. Thorin regards the treasure as his inheritance and plans to fight for it, however, regardless of what the people of Lake Town have suffered.

Under Thorin's orders, the company retreats to the mountain and fortifies it by building a formidable wall at the main gate. From there, they watch as Bard and representatives of the elves approach. Bard informs them that he killed Smaug and that Lake Town has been destroyed. He asks that the dwarves be generous in sharing the wealth of the mountain, since they have benefited so much at the expense of the humans. Thorin flatly refuses. He feels that he owes the humans nothing since the gold belonged to his people originally. Bard gives Thorin some time to reconsider, but Thorin will not change his position. The mountain is declared besieged: nothing and no one will be let in or out if elves and men can help it. Bilbo, for his part, would gladly share the treasure. He is entirely discouraged by the whole turn of affairs. However, no dwarf questions Thorin, and the hobbit has no say in the dwarves' decision.

ANALYSIS: CHAPTERS 14–15

Bard, the only human hero in *The Hobbit,* is grim, courageous, and honorable. Bard's descent from the people of Dale—who lived in peace with Thorin's ancestors in happier times, before Smaug—allows him to hear the words of the thrush that communicates Bilbo's message. Bard is brave enough to be the last man standing in the town and skilled enough to kill Smaug with a shot. Bard is kind and reasonable, presenting the demands of the men and the elves as politely as possible to Thorin and asking only for what is needed to rebuild Lake Town and help alleviate his people's suffering.

After they find the treasure, the dwarves' disturbing greed escalates to the extent that Thorin seems more like a villain than a hero by Chapter 15. We sense that poor Bilbo, as an ally of the dwarves, is stuck on the wrong side of the conflict. When the elf and human armies advance to propose that the treasure be shared, the narrator observes that Thorin's lust for gold has been building ever since he entered the dragon's lair. This lust has made Thorin and most of the other dwarves totally unreasonable. We are told that only Bombur, Fili, and Kili do not completely share Thorin's stubbornness.

More than simply criticizing the dwarf race, Tolkien's depiction of the dwarves' insensitivity also serves as a warning against the destructive power of greed, which has turned those who were once friends—the dwarves under the mountain and the men of Dale—into enemies. Humans, dwarves, and elves who are all "Good People" ought to be on the same side in Middle-Earth, and their common enemy ought to be evil creatures, such as the goblins. Such was the case while the dragon was alive, but now that Smaug is out of the way, lust for gold blurs the proper lines between good and evil.

In a sense, Bilbo's desire for peace and his generous desire to share the treasure is another mark of *The Hobbit*'s swerving between the modern and ancient epic traits that shape his character. Bard's slaying of the dragon is thoroughly drawn from epic literature, but Bilbo's desire for a peaceful outcome to the conflict would be hard to find in Anglo-Saxon literature. In ancient Anglo-Saxon and Scandinavian epics, gold and treasure were treated with the same seriousness and reverence that is exhibited by the dwarves. Though the source of *The Hobbit*'s characters' reverence for gold is different—gold in epic literature is valuable as much for its ability to create social stability as for its purchasing power—the strife that treasure creates mirrors the conflict found in epics like *Beowulf*. Bilbo's desire for understanding and sharing is a sign that, having explored epic heroism both in Bilbo's past actions and in Bard's slaying of Smaug, Tolkien is also interested in exploring a more modern notion of heroism, which connects courage to sympathy and understanding.

CHAPTERS 16–17

SUMMARY: CHAPTER 16

As Thorin continues to search for the Arkenstone and as the rest of the dwarves worry about the armies camped on their doorstep, Bilbo decides that he must take matters into his own hands. With the help of the ring, he sneaks away from the mountain at night and into the camp of the lake men and the wood elves. There, he reveals himself and is brought before the leaders, Bard and the Elvenking. They are suspicious of him, of course, but they relax when Bilbo reveals his secret weapon: the Arkenstone. He gives it freely to Bard to be used as a bargaining chip against Thorin. Bard and the Elvenking are amazed that the hobbit would risk inciting the anger of the dwarves in order to prevent a war. They ask him to stay in the camp for his safety, but Bilbo decides to return to the mountain. On his way out of the camp, he runs into Gandalf, who pats him on the shoulder for his brave deeds. Gandalf has just arrived from his other affairs to see the end of this touchy matter. Newly hopeful, Bilbo sneaks back to the mountain unnoticed.

SUMMARY: CHAPTER 17

In the morning, Bard returns with two messengers to entreat Thorin to accept a peaceable agreement. When the dwarf again refuses, Bard reveals the Arkenstone, the one part of the treasure that Thorin values above all the rest. Thorin is crushed, and he turns to Bilbo in rage when the hobbit reveals that he is the one who gave Bard the treasure. Thorin is about to turn violent, but then one of the messengers throws off his cloak and reveals himself to be Gandalf.

The wizard commands Thorin to let Bilbo speak. The hobbit claims that, in taking the Arkenstone, he only took his fair share of the treasure, as his contract as burglar had specified. Thorin has no choice but to agree, and he angrily offers to pay a fourteenth part of the treasure to regain the stone. The men and elves are satisfied with this. Thorin, however, secretly hopes that before they make the exchange, his relatives, who are marching toward the battlefield with an army under the leadership of Dain, will be able to capture the stone by force.

The new dwarf army threatens the elves and men, and they are about to engage in battle when darkness takes over the sky from the west. Gandalf tells them that a new danger has come: an army of goblins and Wargs who intend to take the treasure for themselves. The dwarves, elves, and humans are thus united against the goblins and Wargs in what is called the Battle of the Five Armies.

The forces of good fight fiercely, but the goblins and Wargs are just as fierce. Bilbo stays on the mountain, a bit removed from the fighting, and watches as the elves and dwarves first send the goblins fleeing but then are forced to retreat from the vicious Wargs. Thorin fights alongside the lake men as mightily as any. However, the goblins slowly gain ground, and Bilbo is forced to retreat to the elves' camp, which is nearly surrounded. The end seems close at hand when the hobbit's keen eyes spy something in the distant skies: the great eagles are flying toward the battlefield. At that moment, however, a stone falls from the mountain and hits Bilbo on the head, and he loses consciousness.

ANALYSIS: CHAPTERS 16–17

In this section, the idea Tolkien began developing in Chapter 15— that the dwarves are in the wrong and that the truly heroic path is the one that ends in peace—comes to fruition with Bilbo's moral choice to leave the dwarves. Bilbo's motivations for defecting to the enemy camp are twofold. First, he realizes that the best way out of the conflict is a peaceful one. Second, despite his friendship with the dwarves, Bilbo feels more of a natural camaraderie with elves (and, to a lesser extent, with men) than with dwarves. Though this second motivation may be questioned, Bilbo's defection is nevertheless one of the most courageous acts of his short career as a burglar, since without Gandalf's intervention he may easily have been killed by Thorin for giving away the Arkenstone.

Bilbo's defection also develops the strain of modern heroism in the novel, as opposed to the strain of heroism based on epic literature. Loyalty to one's lord and solidarity to one's group are among the paramount virtues in epic literature, but Bilbo abandons those virtues by making an independent moral choice, designed to create the best outcome rather than the outcome willed by his lord, Thorin. Tolkien further critiques the idea of unquestioned loyalty by emphasizing Thorin's pigheadedness and bad behavior.

The moral hierarchy of race that has been developed throughout *The Hobbit* is brought into sharp relief with the arrival of the goblins and the Wargs. The appearance of these truly evil races forces the essentially good creatures to band together, as the armies line up according to fundamental divisions between good and evil, rather than according to claims for money. Certainly, the money is still at stake in the Battle of the Five Armies—it is the reason that the goblins and Wargs have come in the first place—but the more urgent conflict is between good and evil. The dwarves, elves, and men are all "Good People," and, as we see here, this division runs deeper than the family pride of Thorin or even the long-standing feud between dwarves and elves. The alliance of dwarves, men, and elves recalls happier days when the three races were peaceful neighbors and worked together to create great cities.

The goblins', dragons', and other evil creatures' increasing power and their near-victory in the battle signal the fading glory of Middle-Earth. Fortunately for the armies of good, one great race—the eagles—has been preserved almost untouched from the beginning of time. Once again, we see nature taking a side when good and evil clash. The pure eagles would not have intervened in a war over gold, but the involvement of the goblins cries out to their sense of good and brings them down from the mountaintops. Here Tolkien reiterates an essential quality of his fantasy world: evil, characterized by the perversion of nature, may become powerful, but the essential nature of the world is good.

CHAPTERS 18–19

SUMMARY: CHAPTER 18

> *If more of us valued food and cheer and song above hoarded gold, it would be a merrier world.*
> (See QUOTATIONS, p. 44)

When Bilbo awakens, he is still lying with a bad headache on the side of the mountain, but he is otherwise unharmed. From the camps below, he sees that his side has won the battle against the goblins and Wargs. A man comes searching for Bilbo but cannot find him

SUMMARY & ANALYSIS

until the hobbit remembers to take off his magic ring. Bilbo is carried back to the camp where Gandalf waits and is delighted to see the hobbit alive. However, there is sad business to attend to. Bilbo must say farewell to Thorin, who is mortally wounded. Thorin asks Bilbo's forgiveness for the harsh words spoken earlier.

Fili and Kili have also been killed, but the rest of the dwarves have survived. Gandalf describes the end of the battle for Bilbo: the eagles, watching the movements of the goblins, came just in time and turned the tide of battle. Yet things still might have gone badly were it not for the sudden appearance of Beorn in the shape of a bear, massive and enraged. This sent the rest of the goblins scattering, and now they are all either dead or in hiding.

SUMMARY: CHAPTER 19

The dead are buried, and Dain is crowned the new King under the Mountain. The dwarves are at peace with the lake men and the wood elves. Bard is the new Master of Lake Town, and from his share of the treasure, he gives Bilbo a handsome sum. Soon, it is time for the hobbit to return home. He travels with Gandalf and Beorn, taking the long way north around Mirkwood, for nothing could persuade him to enter that forest again. They spend most of the harsh winter at Beorn's house, with much feasting and merriment.

In the spring, they continue on to Rivendell. There, Gandalf and Elrond exchange many tales of great deeds, past and present, while Bilbo recovers from his weariness and wounds through rest and the magic of the elves. Bilbo learns the reason Gandalf left the company near Mirkwood: he was fighting alongside the council of wizards to drive the Necromancer out of the forest. Finally, Bilbo and Gandalf travel the last, long stretch of road back to the hobbit lands. Approaching his home, Bilbo receives a nasty surprise. He has been presumed dead, and the contents of his hill are being auctioned off.

Though he puts a stop to the auction and recovers most of his valuables, Bilbo is never again really accepted by the other hobbits. They view his adventuring with skepticism, and his return with gold and tales of dragons and war only confirms the hobbits' suspicion that Bilbo has gotten in over his head. This Bilbo doesn't mind—now that he has a wizard, elves, and the occasional dwarf coming to visit him, he does not care much for the company of respectable hobbits. Most important, however, he still has his kettle, his pipe, and all the comforts of his home at Bag End.

ANALYSIS: CHAPTERS 18–19

Thorin's parting words resolve *The Hobbit*'s central conflict. Thorin at last regrets his greed, and he recognizes the value of a race like the hobbits (and particularly of Bilbo), which he had scorned at the beginning of the book. "If more of us valued food and cheer and song above hoarded gold, it would be a merrier world," Thorin says. Bilbo's love of food, cheer, and song seem like undesirable qualities when we first meet him in his hill at Bag End. However, the great elves share these qualities, while the ill-fated Thorin does not.

Throughout *The Hobbit*, Bilbo struggles to subdue his love of comfort, which is the product of his Baggins heritage, and to tune in to his love of adventure, which comes from his Took heritage. However, he never really loses touch with the Baggins in him. As he rests in Beorn's house, we see a return to the Bilbo who wishes nothing more than to sit in his old armchair. If *The Hobbit* has an overarching message, it is that even a small, unassuming person such as Bilbo possesses the inner resources necessary to perform adventurous, heroic deeds and that the transformation that makes him a hero does not erase his essential nature.

Bilbo's heroic deeds are all the more remarkable because they fail to change him. He possesses a new confidence and a drastically widened perspective on the world, to the point that he now prefers the company of elves and wizards to that of other hobbits. Much of *The Hobbit* explores the contrast between the world in ancient epics that Tolkien studied as a scholar and the modern, English world in which he lived. The novel closes with a compromise between the two worlds: Bilbo goes on living amid the comforts of Bag End, but he passes his time reading and writing about adventure and conversing with characters from his heroic quest. In a way, this image is a concise symbol of Tolkien himself, living his comfortable life at Oxford while immersed in the grim violent imaginative realm of heroic literature, which he both studied and wrote.

The company's quest, which seemed tainted by the greed that motivated it, is redeemed by its wide-ranging and beneficial effects. Lake Town is rebuilt stronger than before. Humans can once again live in Dale, no longer fearing the dragon's fire. The goblins have been conquered, and, thus, much of the wilderness of the east has been made safer for travelers. Moreover, Bilbo hears in Rivendell that the errand that Gandalf performed while he was away from the quest was to join a great council of wizards, who have succeeded in driving the Necromancer out of southern Mirkwood. This is another incident that will have important ramifications in *The Lord of the Rings,* as the dark lord merely leaves Mirkwood to return to his ancient stronghold in the land of Mordor, where he attempts to conquer the world.

Despite our sense that other, perhaps grander, adventures are happening at the same time as the events recounted in *The Hobbit,* Bilbo nevertheless ends up playing a significant role in the larger affairs of Middle-Earth. Certainly, without Bilbo's intervention at several tough points, Smaug would never have been killed, the treasure would never have been recovered, and the goblins would still roam the Misty Mountains. He is without question a hero, although such a title would hardly suit his tastes. In the book's last passage, Gandalf jokingly chides the hobbit about his insignificance, telling him that he is "only quite a little fellow in a wide world after all!" In part, the wizard is laughing at himself, because even he could hardly have foreseen just how important a role Bilbo would play.

SUMMARY & ANALYSIS

Important Quotations Explained

1. "Let's have no more argument. I have chosen Mr. Baggins and that ought to be enough for all of you. If I say he is a Burglar, a Burglar he is, or will be when the time comes. There is a lot more in him than you guess, and a deal more than he has any idea of himself. You may (possibly) all live to thank me yet."

Gandalf speaks these words in Chapter 1 shortly after Bilbo faints from terror at the prospect of going on the quest with the dwarves. After Bilbo's display of fear, the dwarves are skeptical that Bilbo will make a good addition to the party, and Gandalf gives this speech to ease their doubts. The speech is important both because it exemplifies Gandalf's habit of insisting that his own authority be taken as definitive proof and also because it foreshadows Bilbo's transformation into a hero. The trajectory of the novel from this point forward essentially involves Bilbo's discovery of the "lot more in him" that even he does not yet know.

2. "It's got to ask uss a question, my preciouss, yes, yess, yess. Jusst one more question to guess, yes, yess."

Gollum speaks these words during his riddle game with Bilbo in Chapter 5. These sentences perfectly capture Gollum's corrupt, sibilant, hissing form of speech. He never addresses Bilbo directly but speaks only to his mysterious "precious," calling Bilbo "It." Gollum's infatuation with his precious also acts as a bit of foreshadowing. "Precious" turns out to be the magic ring that Bilbo had discovered and placed in his pocket. Gollum's devotion to the ring highlights its extreme, seductive powers.

3. "Somehow [after] the killing of this giant spider, all alone
by himself in the dark . . . made a great difference to Mr.
Baggins. He felt a different person, and much fiercer and
bolder in spite of an empty stomach, as he wiped his sword
on the grass and put it back into its sheath. 'I will give you
a name,' he said to it, 'and I shall call you Sting.'"

This passage from Chapter 8 depicts Bilbo's reaction to his narrow
escape from the giant spider of Mirkwood, one of the novel's major turning points. Defeating a foe in combat gives Bilbo a taste of
the confidence that he has not previously enjoyed, making him feel
"much fiercer and bolder in spite of an empty stomach." From this
point forward, Bilbo shows that he is capable of taking the initiative
and acting in the best interest of the company rather than his own
self-interest, as his ability to ignore his hunger shows. He upstages
Thorin as a leader and establishes himself as a hero.

Bilbo's decision to name his sword is also symbolic. Named
swords are marks of reputation and prowess in ancient epic literature, and Bilbo's naming of his sword essentially represents his lay-
ing claim to the mantle of heroism.

4. "The most that can be said for the dwarves is this: they
intended to pay Bilbo really handsomely for his services;
they had brought him to do a nasty job for them, and they
did not mind the poor little fellow doing it if he would;
but they would all have done their best to get him out of
trouble, if he got into it. . . . There it is: dwarves are not
heroes, but calculating folk with a great idea of the value
of money; some are tricky and treacherous and pretty
bad lots; some are not, but are decent enough people like
Thorin and Company, if you don't expect too much."

In this passage from Chapter 12, the narrator makes an apology for
the dwarves' bad behavior in sending Bilbo into the dragon's lair all
alone. The narrator implies that the dwarves' cowardice is not really their fault. Their character—their greed and deceptiveness—is
inherent to their race. Tolkien's apologetic explanation indicates the
extent to which race is treated as a powerful determinant of identity
in his Middle-Earth. No character is capable of breaking past the

boundaries set by birth—goblins are all evil, elves are all good, and so on. It is important to note, however, that race in Middle-Earth is not the same as race in the real world.

5. "There is more in you of good than you know, child of the kindly West. Some courage and some wisdom, blended in measure. If more of us valued food and cheer and song above hoarded gold, it would be a merrier world."

Thorin speaks these words in Chapter 18, just before he dies, asking Bilbo's forgiveness for his harsh words to him before the Battle of the Five Armies. Thorin acknowledges that, though in his greed he has looked on Bilbo's simple goodness with contempt, the world would be a better place with more Bilbos and fewer Thorins. This quotation places the book's contrast between the simple life of modernity and the grim heroism of the ancient epic in a new light. Bilbo initially felt that the rigors of heroism would force him to abandon the complacency of his simple life at Hobbiton. At the conclusion of the novel, we see that if everyone led a simple, hobbitlike life, the world would be free of evil, and heroism would, in effect, be unnecessary. This new understanding lies behind Bilbo's decision to return to Hobbiton at the end of the book and is Tolkien's closing moral position in *The Hobbit*.

KEY FACTS

FULL TITLE
The Hobbit, or *There and Back Again*

AUTHOR
J. R. R. Tolkien

TYPE OF WORK
Novel

GENRE
Fantasy, heroic quest, satire, comic epic, children's story

LANGUAGE
English

TIME AND PLACE WRITTEN
Roughly between 1929 and 1936 in Oxford, England; since the story was first told orally to Tolkien's children, there is some doubt as to the exact dates of its composition.

DATE OF FIRST PUBLICATION
1937

PUBLISHER
Houghton Mifflin

NARRATOR
The anonymous narrator is playful and humorous. He tends to speak in a comic voice with frequent asides and humorous descriptions of the characters. Bilbo, for instance, is often called Mr. Baggins or "the poor little fellow."

POINT OF VIEW
The novel is narrated in the third person, almost exclusively from Bilbo's point of view. The narration is omniscient, which means that the narrator not only relates Bilbo's thoughts and feelings but also comments on them.

TONE
The narrator's tone is light and casual, and he encourages his readers not to take his story too seriously by making frequent jokes at his characters' expense. The narrator's tone periodically

becomes darker when the company faces great danger or defeat (as in the chapters taking place in Mirkwood), but for the most part, the story is brightly and warmly narrated.

TENSE
Past

SETTING (TIME)
The Third Age of Middle-Earth, 2941–2942

SETTINGS (PLACE)
Various locales in the imaginary world of Middle-Earth

PROTAGONIST
Bilbo Baggins, a hobbit

MAJOR CONFLICT
Bilbo's timidity, complacency, and uncertainty work against his inner strength and heroism. As he travels and embarks on adventures, he must gradually learn to rely on his own abilities and to take the initiative to do what he feels is right.

RISING ACTION
Gandalf visits Bilbo and orders him to act as the burglar for the dwarves' expedition to regain Thorin's treasure from Smaug. Bilbo reluctantly departs, and with each increasingly difficult adventure, he accepts more responsibility for the welfare of the group.

CLIMAX
After Bilbo kills a spider in Chapter 8, he finally has enough confidence in his own abilities as a leader and hero. The Battle of the Five Armies in Chapter 17 is the climax of the expedition.

FALLING ACTION
Bilbo and Gandalf begin the journey home after regaining the treasure, resolving the differences between the dwarves, elves, and men, and defeating the Wargs and goblins. They first spend time with Beorn, then sojourn in Rivendell before returning to Hobbiton. Bilbo has a newfound appreciation for the comforts of his dwelling, but he recognizes that his view of society and his surroundings has undergone profound change.

THEMES
Bilbo's heroism; race, lineage, and character

MOTIFS

Contrasting worldviews, the nature and geography of Middle-Earth

SYMBOLS

Named swords, hobbits

FORESHADOWING

The description of Bilbo's Took blood; Gandalf's insistence that there is more to Bilbo than meets the eye; Gollum's addresses to his mysterious "precious"; Beorn's warnings not to leave the path in Mirkwood; the thrush's interest in Bilbo's description of Smaug's weakness

STUDY QUESTIONS

1.   *Is Thorin in any sense a heroic leader? Do his actions in
      the novel make him deserving of his death at the end?*

By the time the Battle of the Five Armies commences, Thorin has
incurred the contempt and disrespect of many of the book's characters (and probably most readers). But to Thorin's credit, he shows
tremendous courage in attempting to reclaim his ancestors' treasure
from Smaug. We come to learn that his failings—which become
apparent once he is inside the Lonely Mountain—are common to
all dwarves, who possess a great desire for gold and a fierce, even
arrogant pride.

Thorin's great crime is his ingratitude toward his benefactors, the
many lake men who died so that Smaug could be killed. Thorin's
stubbornness over the legitimate ownership of the gold is dishon-
orable and costs lives, but he strives to redeem himself in the end
by admitting his mistakes to Bilbo. Still, it is not really possible to
consider Thorin a hero. He lacks the capacity to formulate and ex-
ecute plans, and he relies on Bilbo to get him through nearly every
difficulty he encounters.

2.   *Given his development throughout the book, does
      Bilbo belong in Hobbiton at the end of the novel? He
      is not completely accepted by the hobbit community,
      but he seems to be perfectly happy there. How do you
      think Tolkien views the relationship between heroism
      and the simple life?*

At the beginning of the novel, the simple life seems antithetical to heroism, but by the end of the novel, after Bilbo has proven his common
sense and courage, his resumption of the simple life seems like a small
act of heroism in itself. Thorin comments that if more of the conten-
tious warriors of the world lived the way hobbits do, it would be a
happier world, and Bilbo's return to Hobbiton seems an acknowl-
edgment of the same idea. Heroism is important in a world beset
with evil, but Tolkien suggests that if everyone lived the simple life of
hobbits, evil would be obsolete. So, in a sense, Bilbo does belong in
Hobbiton, even if he does not in the eyes of the hobbit community.

3.   *Where do humans fit in among the other races of*
     Middle-Earth? Are humans a "good" race?

As we have seen, the various races portrayed in Middle-Earth each demonstrate very specific invariable characteristics. Human goodness does vary, however. Tolkien shows that in the human race, each individual determines his or her goodness. Bard, for instance, is a hero and a kind man, though grim. But the old Master of Lake Town is greedy and manipulative in an almost pitiful way—he dies out in the desert, clutching gold stolen from the town. Humans seem to be more often good than bad but mostly somewhere in the middle. The elves are the truly good race, and the goblins the truly evil one. Humans can match either race in kind but rarely in degree.

How to Write Literary Analysis

The Literary Essay: A Step-by-Step Guide

When you read for pleasure, your only goal is enjoyment. You might find yourself reading to get caught up in an exciting story, to learn about an interesting time or place, or just to pass time. Maybe you're looking for inspiration, guidance, or a reflection of your own life. There are as many different, valid ways of reading a book as there are books in the world.

When you read a work of literature in an English class, however, you're being asked to read in a special way: you're being asked to perform *literary analysis*. To analyze something means to break it down into smaller parts and then examine how those parts work, both individually and together. Literary analysis involves examining all the parts of a novel, play, short story, or poem—elements such as character, setting, tone, and imagery—and thinking about how the author uses those elements to create certain effects.

A literary essay isn't a book review: you're not being asked whether or not you liked a book or whether you'd recommend it to another reader. A literary essay also isn't like the kind of book report you wrote when you were younger, where your teacher wanted you to summarize the book's action. A high school- or college-level literary essay asks, "How does this piece of literature actually work?" "How does it do what it does?" and, "Why might the author have made the choices he or she did?"

The Seven Steps

No one is born knowing how to analyze literature; it's a skill you learn and a process you can master. As you gain more practice with this kind of thinking and writing, you'll be able to craft a method that works best for you. But until then, here are seven basic steps to writing a well-constructed literary essay:

1. *Ask questions*
2. *Collect evidence*
3. *Construct a thesis*

4. Develop and organize arguments
5. Write the introduction
6. Write the body paragraphs
7. Write the conclusion

---

1. Ask Questions

When you're assigned a literary essay in class, your teacher will often provide you with a list of writing prompts. Lucky you! Now all you have to do is choose one. Do yourself a favor and pick a topic that interests you. You'll have a much better (not to mention easier) time if you start off with something you enjoy thinking about. If you are asked to come up with a topic by yourself, though, you might start to feel a little panicked. Maybe you have too many ideas—or none at all. Don't worry. Take a deep breath and start by asking yourself these questions:

- **What struck you?** Did a particular image, line, or scene linger in your mind for a long time? If it fascinated you, chances are you can draw on it to write a fascinating essay.

- **What confused you?** Maybe you were surprised to see a character act in a certain way, or maybe you didn't understand why the book ended the way it did. Confusing moments in a work of literature are like a loose thread in a sweater: if you pull on it, you can unravel the entire thing. Ask yourself why the author chose to write about that character or scene the way he or she did and you might tap into some important insights about the work as a whole.

- **Did you notice any patterns?** Is there a phrase that the main character uses constantly or an image that repeats throughout the book? If you can figure out how that pattern weaves through the work and what the significance of that pattern is, you've almost got your entire essay mapped out.

- **Did you notice any contradictions or ironies?** Great works of literature are complex; great literary essays recognize and explain those complexities. Maybe the title (*Happy Days*) totally disagrees with the book's subject matter (hungry orphans dying in the woods). Maybe the main character acts one way around his family and a completely different way around his friends and associates. If you can find a way to explain a work's contradictory elements, you've got the seeds of a great essay.

At this point, you don't need to know exactly what you're going to say about your topic; you just need a place to begin your exploration. You can help direct your reading and brainstorming by formulating your topic as a *question,* which you'll then try to answer in your essay. The best questions invite critical debates and discussions, not just a rehashing of the summary. Remember, you're looking for something you can *prove or argue* based on evidence you find in the text. Finally, remember to keep the scope of your question in mind: is this a topic you can adequately address within the word or page limit you've been given? Conversely, is this a topic big enough to fill the required length?

GOOD QUESTIONS

"Are Romeo and Juliet's parents responsible for the deaths of their children?"

"Why do pigs keep showing up in LORD OF THE FLIES?*"*

"Are Dr. Frankenstein and his monster alike? How?"

BAD QUESTIONS

"What happens to Scout in TO KILL A MOCKINGBIRD?*"*

"What do the other characters in JULIUS CAESAR *think about Caesar?"*

"How does Hester Prynne in THE SCARLET LETTER *remind me of my sister?"*

---

2. COLLECT EVIDENCE

Once you know what question you want to answer, it's time to scour the book for things that will help you answer the question. Don't worry if you don't know what you want to say yet—right now you're just collecting ideas and material and letting it all percolate. Keep track of passages, symbols, images, or scenes that deal with your topic. Eventually, you'll start making connections between these examples and your thesis will emerge.

Here's a brief summary of the various parts that compose each and every work of literature. These are the elements that you will analyze in your essay, and which you will offer as evidence to support your arguments. For more on the parts of literary works, see the Glossary of Literary Terms at the end of this section.

ELEMENTS OF STORY   These are the *what*s of the work—what happens, where it happens, and to whom it happens.

- **Plot:** All of the events and actions of the work.
- **Character:** The people who act and are acted upon in a literary work. The main character of a work is known as the *protagonist*.
- **Conflict:** The central tension in the work. In most cases, the protagonist wants something, while opposing forces (antagonists) hinder the protagonist's progress.
- **Setting:** When and where the work takes place. Elements of setting include location, time period, time of day, weather, social atmosphere, and economic conditions.
- **Narrator:** The person telling the story. The narrator may straightforwardly report what happens, convey the subjective opinions and perceptions of one or more characters, or provide commentary and opinion in his or her own voice.
- **Themes:** The main idea or message of the work—usually an abstract idea about people, society, or life in general. A work may have many themes, which may be in tension with one another.

ELEMENTS OF STYLE   These are the *how*s—how the characters speak, how the story is constructed, and how language is used throughout the work.

- **Structure and organization:** How the parts of the work are assembled. Some novels are narrated in a linear, chronological fashion, while others skip around in time. Some plays follow a traditional three- or five-act structure, while others are a series of loosely connected scenes. Some authors deliberately leave gaps in their works, leaving readers to puzzle out the missing information. A work's structure and organization can tell you a lot about the kind of message it wants to convey.
- **Point of view:** The perspective from which a story is told. In *first-person point of view,* the narrator involves him or herself in the story. ("I went to the store"; "We watched in horror as the bird slammed into the window.") A first-person narrator is usually the protagonist of the work, but not always. In *third-person point of view,* the narrator does not participate

in the story. A third-person narrator may closely follow a specific character, recounting that individual character's thoughts or experiences, or it may be what we call an *omniscient* narrator. Omniscient narrators see and know all: they can witness any event in any time or place and are privy to the inner thoughts and feelings of all characters. Remember that the narrator and the author are not the same thing!

- **Diction:** Word choice. Whether a character uses dry, clinical language or flowery prose with lots of exclamation points can tell you a lot about his or her attitude and personality.

- **Syntax:** Word order and sentence construction. Syntax is a crucial part of establishing an author's narrative voice. Ernest Hemingway, for example, is known for writing in very short, straightforward sentences, while James Joyce characteristically wrote in long, incredibly complicated lines.

- **Tone:** The mood or feeling of the text. Diction and syntax often contribute to the tone of a work. A novel written in short, clipped sentences that use small, simple words might feel brusque, cold, or matter-of-fact.

- **Imagery:** Language that appeals to the senses, representing things that can be seen, smelled, heard, tasted, or touched.

- **Figurative language:** Language that is not meant to be interpreted literally. The most common types of figurative language are *metaphors* and *similes,* which compare two unlike things in order to suggest a similarity between them— for example, "All the world's a stage," or "The moon is like a ball of green cheese." (Metaphors say one thing *is* another thing; similes claim that one thing is *like* another thing.)

---

3. CONSTRUCT A THESIS

When you've examined all the evidence you've collected and know how you want to answer the question, it's time to write your thesis statement. A *thesis* is a claim about a work of literature that needs to be supported by evidence and arguments. The thesis statement is the heart of the literary essay, and the bulk of your paper will be spent trying to prove this claim. A good thesis will be:

- **Arguable.** "*The Great Gatsby* describes New York society in the 1920s" isn't a thesis—it's a fact.

- **Provable through textual evidence**. "*Hamlet* is a confusing but ultimately very well-written play" is a weak thesis because it offers the writer's personal opinion about the book. Yes, it's arguable, but it's not a claim that can be proved or supported with examples taken from the play itself.

- **Surprising**. "Both George and Lenny change a great deal in *Of Mice and Men*" is a weak thesis because it's obvious. A really strong thesis will argue for a reading of the text that is not immediately apparent.

- **Specific**. "Dr. Frankenstein's monster tells us a lot about the human condition" is *almost* a really great thesis statement, but it's still too vague. What does the writer mean by "a lot"? *How* does the monster tell us so much about the human condition?

GOOD THESIS STATEMENTS

Question: In *Romeo and Juliet*, which is more powerful in shaping the lovers' story: fate or foolishness?

Thesis: "Though Shakespeare defines Romeo and Juliet as 'star-crossed lovers' and images of stars and planets appear throughout the play, a closer examination of that celestial imagery reveals that the stars are merely witnesses to the characters' foolish activities and not the causes themselves."

Question: How does the bell jar function as a symbol in Sylvia Plath's *The Bell Jar*?

Thesis: "A bell jar is a bell-shaped glass that has three basic uses: to hold a specimen for observation, to contain gases, and to maintain a vacuum. The bell jar appears in each of these capacities in *The Bell Jar*, Plath's semi-autobiographical novel, and each appearance marks a different stage in Esther's mental breakdown."

Question: Would Piggy in *The Lord of the Flies* make a good island leader if he were given the chance?

Thesis: "Though the intelligent, rational, and innovative Piggy has the mental characteristics of a good leader, he ultimately lacks the social skills necessary to be an effective one. Golding emphasizes this point by giving Piggy a foil in the charismatic Jack, whose magnetic personality allows him to capture and wield power effectively, if not always wisely."

LITERARY ANALYSIS

4. DEVELOP AND ORGANIZE ARGUMENTS

The reasons and examples that support your thesis will form the middle paragraphs of your essay. Since you can't really write your thesis statement until you know how you'll structure your argument, you'll probably end up working on steps 3 and 4 at the same time.

There's no single method of argumentation that will work in every context. One essay prompt might ask you to compare and contrast two characters, while another asks you to trace an image through a given work of literature. These questions require different kinds of answers and therefore different kinds of arguments. Below, we'll discuss three common kinds of essay prompts and some strategies for constructing a solid, well-argued case.

TYPES OF LITERARY ESSAYS

- **Compare and contrast**

    Compare and contrast the characters of Huck and Jim in THE ADVENTURES OF HUCKLEBERRY FINN.

    Chances are you've written this kind of essay before. In an academic literary context, you'll organize your arguments the same way you would in any other class. You can either go *subject by subject* or *point by point*. In the former, you'll discuss one character first and then the second. In the latter, you'll choose several traits (attitude toward life, social status, images and metaphors associated with the character) and devote a paragraph to each. You may want to use a mix of these two approaches—for example, you may want to spend a paragraph a piece broadly sketching Huck's and Jim's personalities before transitioning into a paragraph or two that describes a few key points of comparison. This can be a highly effective strategy if you want to make a counterintuitive argument—that, despite seeming to be totally different, the two objects being compared are actually similar in a very important way (or vice versa). Remember that your essay should reveal something fresh or unexpected about the text, so think beyond the obvious parallels and differences.

- **Trace**

    Choose an image—for example, birds, knives, or eyes—and trace that image throughout MACBETH.

    Sounds pretty easy, right? All you need to do is read the play, underline every appearance of a knife in *Macbeth,* and then list them in your essay in the order they appear, right? Well, not exactly. Your teacher doesn't want a simple catalog of examples. He or she wants to see you make *connections* between those examples—that's the difference between summarizing and analyzing. In the *Macbeth* example above, think about the different contexts in which knives appear in the play and to what effect. In *Macbeth*, there are real knives and imagined knives; knives that kill and knives that simply threaten. Categorize and classify your examples to give them some order. Finally, always keep the overall effect in mind. After you choose and analyze your examples, you should come to some greater understanding about the work, as well as your chosen image, symbol, or phrase's role in developing the major themes and stylistic strategies of that work.

• **Debate**

Is the society depicted in 1984 good for its citizens?

In this kind of essay, you're being asked to debate a moral, ethical, or aesthetic issue regarding the work. You might be asked to judge a character or group of characters (*Is Caesar responsible for his own demise?*) or the work itself (*Is* JANE EYRE *a feminist novel?*). For this kind of essay, there are two important points to keep in mind. First, don't simply base your arguments on your personal feelings and reactions. Every literary essay expects you to read and analyze the work, so search for evidence in the text. What do characters in *1984* have to say about the government of Oceania? What images does Orwell use that might give you a hint about his attitude toward the government? As in any debate, you also need to make sure that you define all the necessary terms before you begin to argue your case. What does it mean to be a "good" society? What makes a novel "feminist"? You should define your terms right up front, in the first paragraph after your introduction.

Second, remember that strong literary essays make contrary and surprising arguments. Try to think outside the box. In the *1984* example above, it seems like the obvious answer would be no, the totalitarian society depicted in Orwell's novel is *not* good for its citizens. But can you think of any arguments for the opposite side? Even if your final assertion is that the novel depicts a cruel, repressive, and therefore harmful society, acknowledging and responding to the counterargument will strengthen your overall case.

LITERARY ANALYSIS

5. WRITE THE INTRODUCTION

Your introduction sets up the entire essay. It's where you present your topic and articulate the particular issues and questions you'll be addressing. It's also where you, as the writer, introduce yourself to your readers. A persuasive literary essay immediately establishes its writer as a knowledgeable, authoritative figure.

An introduction can vary in length depending on the overall length of the essay, but in a traditional five-paragraph essay it should be no longer than one paragraph. However long it is, your introduction needs to:

- **Provide any necessary context.** Your introduction should situate the reader and let him or her know what to expect. What book are you discussing? Which characters? What topic will you be addressing?

- **Answer the "So what?" question.** Why is this topic important, and why is your particular position on the topic noteworthy? Ideally, your introduction should pique the reader's interest by suggesting how your argument is surprising or otherwise counterintuitive. Literary essays make unexpected connections and reveal less-than-obvious truths.

- **Present your thesis.** This usually happens at or very near the end of your introduction.

- **Indicate the shape of the essay to come.** Your reader should finish reading your introduction with a good sense of the scope of your essay as well as the path you'll take toward proving your thesis. You don't need to spell out every step, but you do need to suggest the organizational pattern you'll be using.

Your introduction should not:

- **Be vague.** Beware of the two killer words in literary analysis: *interesting* and *important*. Of course the work, question, or example is interesting and important—that's why you're writing about it!

- **Open with any grandiose assertions.** Many student readers think that beginning their essays with a flamboyant statement such as, "Since the dawn of time, writers have been fascinated with the topic of free will," makes them

THE HOBBIT 🍁 59

sound important and commanding. You know what? It actually sounds pretty amateurish.

- **Wildly praise the work.** Another typical mistake student writers make is extolling the work or author. Your teacher doesn't need to be told that "Shakespeare is perhaps the greatest writer in the English language." You can mention a work's reputation in passing—by referring to *The Adventures of Huckleberry Finn* as "Mark Twain's enduring classic," for example—but don't make a point of bringing it up unless that reputation is key to your argument.

- **Go off-topic.** Keep your introduction streamlined and to the point. Don't feel the need to throw in all kinds of bells and whistles in order to impress your reader—just get to the point as quickly as you can, without skimping on any of the required steps.

---

6. WRITE THE BODY PARAGRAPHS

Once you've written your introduction, you'll take the arguments you developed in step 4 and turn them into your body paragraphs. The organization of this middle section of your essay will largely be determined by the argumentative strategy you use, but no matter how you arrange your thoughts, your body paragraphs need to do the following:

- **Begin with a strong topic sentence.** Topic sentences are like signs on a highway: they tell the reader where they are and where they're going. A good topic sentence not only alerts readers to what issue will be discussed in the following paragraph but also gives them a sense of what argument will be made *about* that issue. "Rumor and gossip play an important role in *The Crucible*" isn't a strong topic sentence because it doesn't tell us very much. "The community's constant gossiping creates an environment that allows false accusations to flourish" is a much stronger topic sentence— it not only tells us *what* the paragraph will discuss (gossip) but *how* the paragraph will discuss the topic (by showing how gossip creates a set of conditions that leads to the play's climactic action).

- **Fully and completely develop a single thought.** Don't skip around in your paragraph or try to stuff in too much material. Body paragraphs are like bricks: each individual

one needs to be strong and sturdy or the entire structure
will collapse. Make sure you have really proven your point
before moving on to the next one.

- **Use transitions effectively.** Good literary essay writers know
  that each paragraph must be clearly and strongly linked to
  the material around it. Think of each paragraph as a response
  to the one that precedes it. Use transition words and phrases
  such as *however, similarly, on the contrary, therefore,* and
  furthermore to indicate what kind of response you're making.

---

7. WRITE THE CONCLUSION

Just as you used the introduction to ground your readers in the topic
before providing your thesis, you'll use the conclusion to quickly
summarize the specifics learned thus far and then hint at the broader
implications of your topic. A good conclusion will:

- **Do more than simply restate the thesis.** If your thesis argued
  that *The Catcher in the Rye* can be read as a Christian
  allegory, don't simply end your essay by saying, "And that
  is why *The Catcher in the Rye* can be read as a Christian
  allegory." If you've constructed your arguments well, this
  kind of statement will just be redundant.

- **Synthesize the arguments, not summarize them.** Similarly,
  don't repeat the details of your body paragraphs in your
  conclusion. The reader has already read your essay, and
  chances are it's not so long that they've forgotten all your
  points by now.

- **Revisit the "So what?" question.** In your introduction,
  you made a case for why your topic and position are
  important. You should close your essay with the same sort
  of gesture. What do your readers know now that they didn't
  know before? How will that knowledge help them better
  appreciate or understand the work overall?

- **Move from the specific to the general.** Your essay has most
  likely treated a very specific element of the work—a single
  character, a small set of images, or a particular passage. In
  your conclusion, try to show how this narrow discussion has
  wider implications for the work overall. If your essay on *To
  Kill a Mockingbird* focused on the character of Boo Radley,
  for example, you might want to include a bit in your

conclusion about how he fits into the novel's larger message about childhood, innocence, or family life.

- **Stay relevant.** Your conclusion should suggest new directions of thought, but it shouldn't be treated as an opportunity to pad your essay with all the extra, interesting ideas you came up with during your brainstorming sessions but couldn't fit into the essay proper. Don't attempt to stuff in unrelated queries or too many abstract thoughts.

- **Avoid making overblown closing statements.** A conclusion should open up your highly specific, focused discussion, but it should do so without drawing a sweeping lesson about life or human nature. Making such observations may be part of the point of reading, but it's almost always a mistake in essays, where these observations tend to sound overly dramatic or simply silly.

A+ Essay Checklist

Congratulations! If you've followed all the steps we've outlined above, you should have a solid literary essay to show for all your efforts. What if you've got your sights set on an A+? To write the kind of superlative essay that will be rewarded with a perfect grade, keep the following rubric in mind. These are the qualities that teachers expect to see in a truly A+ essay. How does yours stack up?

- ✓ Demonstrates a thorough understanding of the book
- ✓ Presents an original, compelling argument
- ✓ Thoughtfully analyzes the text's formal elements
- ✓ Uses appropriate and insightful examples
- ✓ Structures ideas in a logical and progressive order
- ✓ Demonstrates a mastery of sentence construction, transitions, grammar, spelling, and word choice

SUGGESTED ESSAY TOPICS

1. *What factors define a person's identity in* THE HOBBIT? *Do individuals have any power over who they become, or are their characters entirely determined by static factors such as family and race?*

2. *What is the role of wealth in* THE HOBBIT? *Discuss various characters' attitude toward property and material goods. Whose viewpoint does the novel seem to endorse, if any?*

3. *Describe Tolkien's use of humor in* THE HOBBIT. *From what authorial techniques and sources does the book draw much of its wit? How does Tolkien's lighthearted tone impact the portrayal of the more serious elements of the plot? Is* THE HOBBIT *primarily a comedy?*

A+ Student Essay

> In what ways does *The Hobbit* resemble ancient epic literature? In what ways does it differ? What effect do these connections have on the overall meaning of the novel?

At first glance, *The Hobbit,* with its sweetly cantankerous hero and playful narrative style, does not seem to resemble grim, grand epics such as Beowulf or *The Iliad.* Epic poems feature glorious heroes and are narrated in an elevated style befitting the tale's sober importance. In their grandiosity, the epics that Tolkien studied seem completely unlike the simple adventure story he wrote. However, an examination of *The Hobbit*'s formal elements, such as plot and narrative voice, reveals many points of resemblance between this simple children's novel and the great epics. The critical difference lies in *The Hobbit*'s depiction of its central hero, Bilbo—a creature utterly unlike the traditional heroes of epic literature, whose simple, goodhearted bravery redefines the very notion of a hero.

Though *The Hobbit* is written in a more colloquial, child-friendly style than the classical epics, it makes many nods toward oral storytelling, a key stylistic element of these ancient works. The earliest epics derived from long, sprawling tales told to live audiences, just as *The Hobbit* began as a series of bedtime stories Tolkien told to his children. The novel's oral beginnings are reflected in the frequent comments the narrator directs to the reader, typically soothing reassurances (such as a parent might make to a scared but excited child) that Bilbo and his friends will, in fact, vanquish the foe they are about to encounter. The recurring use of songs further emphasizes the novel's oral nature. Not only do these verses make the novel more fun to read aloud, they also demonstrate how the inhabitants of Middle Earth use music and poems to reinforce community, maintain a sense of history, and commemorate and celebrate notable events.

The Hobbit is structured as a classic quest narrative, a common feature in many ancient epics. In this type of story, a hero sets out to accomplish a dangerous goal, often traveling over the span of his known world in the process and encountering representative samples of its different people. Along the way to achieving his ultimate objective, the protagonist encounters a series of setbacks, each of which constitutes a separate, discrete episode in the narrative.

Not unlike a modern video game, Bilbo and the dwarves must pass several distinct tests—the trolls, the goblins of the Misty Mountains, the giant spiders, and the wood elves of Mirkwood—before they reach the final showdown with Smaug, which represents the culmination of the quest narrative. The dragon as final challenge is a familiar motif in the Anglo-Saxon and Scandinavian epics (*Beowulf* being the most famous example), and the scene features many items commonly found in these stories, such as riddles, named swords, magic objects, and significant talismans. In addition, modest little Bilbo seems to acknowledge his heroic role most decisively in this scene. He announces to Smaug, "I am Ringwinner and Luckwearer; and I am Barrel-rider." The titles Bilbo gives himself recall the heroic epithets—short, descriptive nicknames—commonly found in ancient epic literature, suggesting that Bilbo is starting to think of himself as such a hero.

However, Bilbo doesn't triumph over Smaug in this scene, as we might expect in a traditional tale of heroism. In fact, in these last sections of the novel, the contrast between Bilbo and the archetypal hero becomes even more pronounced. Throughout *The Hobbit*, Bilbo's small stature, down-to-earth nature, and love of comfort have made him an unlikely hero. Epic heroes tend to be nobly or divinely born, possessed of supernatural skill or strength, and preoccupied with fame and glory—none of which applies to Bilbo. In the scene with Smaug, which has been set up as the tale's climactic showdown, Bilbo escapes without attempting to defeat his foe. Eventually it is the human captain, Bard, who finally kills the dragon. Bilbo doesn't even fight in the great Battle of the Five Armies, having been knocked out by a falling stone.

If anyone in *The Hobbit* resembles a traditional hero, it is the grim, courageous Bard, who distinguishes himself both as a warrior and as a wise, sober leader. And in the end, he receives the more traditional heroic rewards: fame, honor, and a high position of power. This is in sharp contrast to Bilbo, who leaves with less treasure than he'd initially been promised and meets with cold suspicion from his fellow hobbits when he finally returns home. However, Bard is never more than a supporting character in this story. Bilbo is clearly the protagonist and hero of *The Hobbit*, and Tolkien suggests that we should honor him as such for very different reasons than ancient Europeans would have honored their heroes. Bilbo's great, final act of heroism doesn't involve military bravery or a feat of physical strength. Rather, it is an act of selflessness: He offers the precious Arkenstone, equivalent to his percentage of the treasure, as a bargaining chip for the humans to negotiate a settlement with the dwarves. Bilbo's dedication to comfort, which seems a small-minded trait, is also what leads to his love of peace and accord. Bilbo may not have defeated the dragon or vanquished the Wargs, but he single-handedly brought unity to the people of the Five Armies, establishing a peaceful coalition that will prove crucial in the subsequent *Lord of the Rings* trilogy. The fact that he rejects the traditional heroic rewards—neither receiving nor requiring fame and glory—only makes him more heroic and admirable.

LITERARY ANALYSIS

GLOSSARY OF LITERARY TERMS

ANTAGONIST

The entity that acts to frustrate the goals of the *protagonist*. The antagonist is usually another *character* but may also be a non-human force.

ANTIHERO / ANTIHEROINE

A *protagonist* who is not admirable or who challenges notions of what should be considered admirable.

CHARACTER

A person, animal, or any other thing with a personality that appears in a *narrative*.

CLIMAX

The moment of greatest intensity in a text or the major turning point in the *plot*.

CONFLICT

The central struggle that moves the *plot* forward. The conflict can be the *protagonist*'s struggle against fate, nature, society, or another person.

FIRST-PERSON POINT OF VIEW

A literary style in which the *narrator* tells the story from his or her own *point of view* and refers to himself or herself as "I." The narrator may be an active participant in the story or just an observer.

HERO / HEROINE

The principal *character* in a literary work or *narrative*.

IMAGERY

Language that brings to mind sense-impressions, representing things that can be seen, smelled, heard, tasted, or touched.

MOTIF

A recurring idea, structure, contrast, or device that develops or informs the major *themes* of a work of literature.

NARRATIVE

A story.

NARRATOR

The person (sometimes a *character*) who tells a story; the *voice* assumed by the writer. The narrator and the author of the work of literature are not the same person.

PLOT

The arrangement of the events in a story, including the sequence in which they are told, the relative emphasis they are given, and the causal connections between events.

POINT OF VIEW

The *perspective* that a *narrative* takes toward the events it describes.

PROTAGONIST

The main *character* around whom the story revolves.

SETTING

The location of a *narrative* in time and space. Setting creates mood or atmosphere.

SUBPLOT

A secondary *plot* that is of less importance to the overall story but may serve as a point of contrast or comparison to the main plot.

SYMBOL

An object, *character,* figure, or color that is used to represent an abstract idea or concept. Unlike an *emblem,* a symbol may have different meanings in different contexts.

SYNTAX

The way the words in a piece of writing are put together to form lines, phrases, or clauses; the basic structure of a piece of writing.

THEME

A fundamental and universal idea explored in a literary work.

TONE

The author's attitude toward the subject or *characters* of a story or poem or toward the reader.

VOICE

An author's individual way of using language to reflect his or her own personality and attitudes. An author communicates voice through *tone, diction,* and *syntax.*

A Note on Plagiarism

Plagiarism—presenting someone else's work as your own—rears its ugly head in many forms. Many students know that copying text without citing it is unacceptable. But some don't realize that even if you're not quoting directly, but instead are paraphrasing or summarizing, *it is plagiarism* unless you cite the source.

Here are the most common forms of plagiarism:

- Using an author's phrases, sentences, or paragraphs without citing the source
- Paraphrasing an author's ideas without citing the source
- Passing off another student's work as your own

How do you steer clear of plagiarism? You should *always* acknowledge all words and ideas that aren't your own by using quotation marks around verbatim text or citations like footnotes and endnotes to note another writer's ideas. For more information on how to give credit when credit is due, ask your teacher for guidance or visit www.sparknotes.com.

REVIEW & RESOURCES

QUIZ

1. What is the name of Bilbo's hillside home?

   A. Bag End
   B. Crookhollow Bend
   C. Brandywine End
   D. Lothlorien

2. What happens to trolls when they are exposed to daylight?

   A. They explode.
   B. Their strength is tripled.
   C. They turn to stone.
   D. They become invisible.

3. What is Gollum's name for his ring?

   A. Darling
   B. Precious
   C. Sting
   D. Goblinkiller

4. Who kills Smaug?

   A. Gandalf
   B. Thorin
   C. Bilbo
   D. Bard

5. Who is the master of Rivendell?

   A. Elrond
   B. Smaug
   C. Gandalf
   D. Celeborn

6. What effect does the magic ring have?

    A. It turns its wearer to stone.
    B. It makes its wearer invisible.
    C. It triples its wearer's strength.
    D. It gives its wearer the power to harness lightning.

7. Where does Bilbo choose to live at the end of the novel?

    A. Rivendell
    B. Lake Town
    C. Mirkwood
    D. His old home at Hobbiton

8. At what university was Tolkien a professor?

    A. Oxford
    B. Yale
    C. Cambridge
    D. UCLA

9. What posthumously published book explains the mythology Tolkien created for Middle-Earth?

    A. *The Lord of the Rings*
    B. *Gawain and the Green Knight*
    C. *The Silmarillion*
    D. *The Lion, the Witch, and the Wardrobe*

10. What is the name of the evil wolflike creatures that support the goblins?

    A. Morlocks
    B. Wargs
    C. Nazgul
    D. Balfrogs

11. What two shapes can Beorn assume?

    A. Human and elk
    B. Bear and hawk
    C. Human and eagle
    D. Human and bear

12. Who stops Thorin from attacking Bilbo?

    A.   Gandalf
    B.   Fili
    C.   Kili
    D.   Bofur

13. What evil sorcerer has taken up residence in Mirkwood?

    A.   The Illusionist
    B.   The Enchanter
    C.   The Necromancer
    D.   The Alchemist

14. What does Bilbo name his sword?

    A.   Glamdring
    B.   Sting
    C.   Bolt
    D.   Slicer

15. What is the name of Gandalf's sword?

    A.   Sting
    B.   Orcrist
    C.   Dicer
    D.   Glamdring

16. Where is Smaug's lair?

    A.   Under the Misty Mountains
    B.   Under the Lonely Mountain
    C.   In the mines of Moria
    D.   Beneath the plains of Rohan

17. What kind of contest do Bilbo and Gollum hold?

    A.   Arm-wrestling
    B.   Singing
    C.   Riddle-solving
    D.   Racing

18. What is Smaug's weakness?

    A.   A missing scale above his heart
    B.   A fear of fire
    C.   A tendency to become depressed in winter
    D.   A fondness for children

19. What is happening to Bilbo's possessions when he returns home?

    A.   They are being burned by goblins.
    B.   They are being stolen.
    C.   They are being used by his neighbors.
    D.   They are being auctioned.

20. Who saves the party from the Wargs?

    A.   The hawks
    B.   The lions
    C.   The moth men
    D.   The eagles

21. Who was Thror?

    A.   Thorin's father
    B.   Thorin's grandfather
    C.   Thorin's uncle
    D.   Bilbo's father

22. What two sides of Bilbo's family define much of his personality?

    A.   Baggins and Brandybuck
    B.   Brandybuck and Took
    C.   Baggins and Took
    D.   Dale and Brandybuck

23. Where does Bilbo hide the dwarves during their escape from the wood elves?

    A.   In barrels
    B.   In wagons
    C.   In chests
    D.   Under the trolls' invisibility spell

24. How old is Gandalf?

    A. 2,200
    B. 68
    C. 230
    D. Gandalf's age is never given

25. What distinguishes a hobbit's feet from human feet?

    A. They are larger.
    B. They smell like pork.
    C. They have clawed toes.
    D. They are woolly.

ANSWER KEY

1: A; 2: C; 3: B; 4: D; 5: A; 6: B; 7: D; 8: A; 9: C; 10: B; 11: D; 12: A;
13: C; 14: B; 15: D; 16: B; 17: C; 18: A; 19: D; 20: D; 21: B; 22: C;
23: A; 24: D; 25: D

GLOSSARY OF TERMS IN *THE HOBBIT*

BAG END
> The hole occupied by the hobbit Bilbo Baggins.

THE BAGGINSES
> A somewhat noble line of hobbits who exemplify the desire of
> hobbits in general. These hobbits, of which Bilbo takes half his
> heritage on his father's side, are well-intentioned and enjoy the
> comforts of home.

BURGLAR
> Bilbo's capacity in the quest to recover the treasure of the
> dragon Smaug. As a hobbit, Bilbo does not seem to fit the part
> of a burglar in the dwarves' schemes, but his unassuming nature
> coupled with his ability to become invisible with the ring he
> takes from Gollum makes him an effective burglar nonetheless.

GLAMDRING
> Gandalf's sword, taken from the trolls in Chapter 2.

HOBBITON
> Bilbo's village. Hobbiton is mentioned only once in this book as
> the name of the place where Bilbo lives, in the last chapter when
> Bilbo's address is given as "Bag-End, Underhill, Hobbiton."
> Although the village is described in depth in *The Lord of the
> Rings* and other Tolkien works, nothing is revealed about it in
> *The Hobbit*.

LAKE TOWN
> A human settlement visited by Bilbo and company in Chapter 10.

LONELY MOUNTAIN
> The whereabouts of Smaug the dragon and his hoard of gold,
> mined by Thorin's grandfather Thror. Lonely Mountain has a
> secret entrance with a secret keyhole, which Elrond discovers as
> he translates runes on weapons and maps.

LONG LAKE
> A body of water near Lake Town. The Long Lake was so "wide
> that the opposite shores looked small and far, but it was so long
> that its northerly end . . . could not be seen at all." The dimen-
> sions of the Long Lake surprised Bilbo because he never knew
> that a body of water that was not the sea could seem as large.

REVIEW & RESOURCES

MIDDLE-EARTH

Tolkien's name for the elaborate fantastical universe he details. The concept of Middle-Earth, which is mentioned frequently throughout this SparkNote, is never mentioned within the text of *The Hobbit*. It is explicit only in *The Lord of the Rings* and *The Silmarillion*.

MIRKWOOD

Woods in Middle-Earth. Mirkwood is the last great obstacle before Lonely Mountain on the path the company takes on its quest. The company meets Beorn, a creature who has a house in the middle of the woods, in Mirkwood, and he offers them food and lodging as well as directions to exit the woods near their destination.

MISTY MOUNTAINS

A range of mountains near the Edge of the Wild. Bilbo and the company of dwarves have to pass the Misty Mountains as part of their quest to the Lonely Mountain and its guarded treasure.

MORIA

A place under the mountains where the mines are located. These are the mines in which Thorin's grandfather Thror labored only to have the dragon Smaug take away the bounty.

ORCRIST

Thorin's sword, taken from the trolls in Chapter 2.

PRECIOUS

Gollum's name for his magic ring, which Bilbo finds and takes.

RIVENDELL

A city of elves located just beyond the Edge of the Wild, near the foothills of the Misty Mountains, Rivendell is the last safe stop along the dwarves' way to the Lonely Mountain.

STING

The eventual name of Bilbo's small sword. Bilbo names the sword Sting after he kills a spider with it, and, thus, accepts his heroism as he honors his weapon by giving it a name like Orcrist or Excalibur.

THE TOOKS

A line of hobbits who find amusement in adventure, unlike most other hobbits, who enjoy the creature comforts of home. Bilbo is half-Took on his mother's side.

REVIEW & RESOURCES

SUGGESTIONS FOR FURTHER READING

CARPENTER, HUMPHREY. *J. R. R. Tolkien: A Biography.* New York: Houghton Mifflin, 2000.

CLARK, GEORGE and DANIEL TIMMONS, eds. *J. R. R. Tolkien and His Literary Resonances: Views of Middle-Earth.* Westport, CT: Greenwood Press, 2000.

GREEN, WILLIAM H. *The Hobbit: A Journey into Maturity.* New York: Twayne Publishers, 1995.

LOBDELL, JARED. *A Tolkien Compass.* Chicago: Open Court Publishing. 2003.

TOLKIEN, CHRISTOPHER. *The History of* THE LORD OF THE RINGS. 4 vols. New York: Mariner Books, 2000.

TOLKIEN, J. R. R. *The Book of Lost Tales: The History of Middle-Earth.* New York: Del Rey, 1992.

———. *The Letters of J. R. R. Tolkien.* New York: Houghton Mifflin, 2000.

———. *The Lord of the Rings.* New York: Houghton Mifflin, 1994.

———. *The Silmarillion.* New York: Houghton Mifflin, reprint edition 2004.